MARIANNE RAGINS

Winning Scholarships for College

◆ AN INSIDER'S GUIDE ◆

An Owl Book

HENRY HOLT AND COMPANY ◆ NEW YORK

Henry Holt and Company, Inc.
Publishers since 1866
115 West 18th Street
New York, New York 10011

Henry Holt ® is a registered trademark of Henry Holt and Company, Inc.

Published in Canada by Fitzhenry & Whiteside Ltd.,
195 Allstate Parkway, Markham, Ontario L3R 4T8.

Library of Congress Cataloging-in-Publication Data
Ragins, Marianne.
Winning scholarships for college : an insider's guide /
    Marianne Ragins. — 1st Owl Book ed.
p.   cm.
"An Owl book."
Includes bibliographical references and index.
1. Scholarships—United States   2. Student aid—United States.   I. Title.
LB2338.R27   1994   94-14173
378.3′4—dc20   CIP

ISBN 0-8050-3072-7

Henry Holt books are available for special promotions and premiums.
For details contact: Director, Special Markets.

First Edition—1994

Designed by Victoria Hartman

Printed in the United States of America
All first editions are printed on acid-free paper.∞
10 9 8 7 6 5 4 3 2 1

To my grandmother and my father,
who can only see my achievements from up above—
this book is dedicated to your memory.

Contents

Acknowledgments

*F*irst, I would like to acknowledge the former principal of Northeast High School, David Dillard, for his dedication to both the school and its students. He called the first reporter when my scholarship totals reached more than $258,000 in funds because he was determined that I receive recognition for my achievements. Without him, my achievements may not have been recognized as widely, or possibly at all. I acknowledge my mother, Laura Ragins, and my entire family for the support that they have given me throughout my life. Furthermore, I acknowledge all of my teachers from elementary, middle, and high school who contributed to my education. Most important, I thank God for nurturing my family and myself, and for the blessings He has bestowed upon us.

Thank you Rose, Gloria, Nett, Greg, and Dutch for helping so much with the first and second editions.

Thanks, Ann. You did a wonderful job.

Stephanie, your covers are beautiful.

To Tracy Sherrod, my editor, thanks for all your suggestions. They were a major improvement.

I would also like to thank the members of Stubbs Chapel Baptist Church, especially my Aunt Sister and Uncle Sammie, for the support they have given me over the years.

Mom, Sha, and Robert, you're the best friends in the world.

To the scholarship judges and program administrators who chose me as a scholarship recipient, thank you very much for giving not only me but many others the chance of a lifetime. I hope there will be many other winners to follow.

Angela, look at the quote for Chapter 11.

To Marie Brown and the staff at Marie Brown Associates, you are some of the most helpful and friendly people I have ever encountered. Thank you for all your help.

To Florida A & M University, I am glad that you were my choice.

I shall be telling this with a sigh
Somewhere ages and ages hence:
Two roads diverged in a wood, and I—
I took the one less traveled by,
And that has made all the difference.

———————

Robert Frost, "The Road Not Taken"

◆

Introduction

*I*f you have picked this book out of the hundreds of choices in the bookstore or the library, you want to attend a college or university and you need money to do so. By choosing *Winning Scholarships for College* you are well on your way to achieving both of those goals. I know because that's the situation I was in a few years ago. I decided to do something about it, and my efforts since have become history. By the first semester of my freshman year in college I had accumulated more than $400,000 in scholarships and monetary awards. In the process of winning these scholarships I gained national attention. Letters began to pour in from all corners of the United States. They all wanted to know: "How did you do it? In response, I wrote a book, of which you are now reading the latest version. Congratulations, *you* have just taken the first step on the road to winning scholarships for college.

Winning Scholarships for College is intended for students of all ages and all circumstances. Whether you are in middle or high school, returning to college, currently enrolled in college, a person with disabilities, or planning to study abroad, this guide will show you how to secure funds for college. It is designed to help locate scholarships in any area that a student resides since scholarship programs differ from region to region, state to state, and community to community. For instance, the information available in the southeastern region, the state of Georgia, and the communities of Macon may not be available elsewhere. In addition, this book offers advice on how to make the best choices when you get scholarship offers from more than one college or university. It suggests ideas on how to look for the best scholarship package, which often includes not only tuition and room and board but also "sweeteners" such as personal-expense stipends. This book will take you beyond any obstacles you may face in your scholarship search. Once you finish it, you will have an excellent understanding of how to secure money in your area for college.

There are several hundred books on the market about winning scholarships but only one like this, because everything written here is coming from the voice of experience. As a scholarship recipient I have experienced the disappointment of rejection, the weariness of constant research, the anxiety of interviews, the joy and the satisfaction of extracurricular activities, the tediousness of applications, the frustration and triumph of writing (or attempting to write) "perfect" essays. This list is by no means complete. But the most essential benefit of all, and one that I hope *you* will soon experience, is the joy of success as you attain goals far beyond your expectations.

The initiative and zeal I displayed by going after scholarship money in high school have ensured that I will never have to worry about undergraduate college expenses. You can be a care-free college student just like me. By reading *Winning Scholarships for College* and employing the strategies I have perfected, coupled with your own initiative and zeal, you will have an unbeatable combination for scholarship success.

As well as leaving your mind free to concentrate on your studies, wouldn't it take a load off your parents' minds and pockets to know your college education is completely paid for? It did for mine. My mother felt as if she were in heaven when she read the letters of award that continuously came in the mail. She was extremely proud of her "baby girl." She also knew, as the letters quickly began to fill up the scrapbook she had started, that she would not have to pay one cent toward my college education.

Guess what? So far she hasn't. In my arrangement with the university I am now attending, Florida Agricultural and Mechanical University, I get enough spending money to handle all of my personal expenses and still have money for Burger King (my favorite hamburger restaurant), the movies, clothes, music, and most anything else I desire. In the past two years the only expense my mother has incurred for my college education has been the postage on the packages she sends from home.

Throughout this book you will find a quotation as a prelude to each chapter. These quotations are meant to set the overall tone for the chapter, stimulate positive insight, and help you find quoted material for essays. The excerpt from the poem by Robert Frost at the beginning of this book contains words that I have used as *my* guiding light for most of my life, even in my search for scholarship money. I saw my quest to find scholarships to attend college as a long journey on a road previously untraveled. I have always taken paths that at the time seemed to be strewn with uncertainty, yet those paths have bestowed the greatest rewards.

Believe it or not, scholarship success can happen for you as well. All it takes is SDP: Self-motivation, Determination, and Persistence. This book outlines my strategies for success and the role that SDP played in my scholarship search. As you begin your personal scholarship journey, remember this: The only place success comes before work is in the dictionary. My equation for success: work + SDP = success. My successful equation totaled well over $400,000. What will yours total?

It worked for me. It can work for you. Good luck!

Books are the quietest and most constant of friends;
they are the most accessible and wisest of counselors,
and the most patient of teachers.

Charles Eliot

◆

1

RESEARCH: DISCOVERING HIDDEN TREASURES

*T*here are many scholarship opportunities available throughout the country. In fact, thousands of scholarship dollars go unclaimed each year because students are not aware they exist. This book shows you how to find those dollars. It also lists programs and addresses that I uncovered during my scholarship search. Yet the addresses I supply should not be used as a substitute for doing your own research. It is most important to know what is available in the state and city in which you live because what's available in one state or city may not be available in another. Also, be knowledgeable of the various sources of financial aid available throughout the United States. If you do not have an idea of the scholarships offered each year, simply because you do not look for them, then you cannot expect to win any of them. Thorough research will reveal many of the opportunities available to you. Without the benefit of extensive research on your part, scholarship dollars that could have been awarded to you will either go unused or go to others who have done their research. Good research, as well as attentive ears and eyes, will be crucial to winning scholarships. Numerous opportunities are waiting for you, but it's your job to discover them.

Here are some terms and facts to make your search easier and less confusing.

- A *scholarship* is money that is given to a student and does not have to be repaid. Scholarships are given for a variety of reasons: academic achievement, leadership potential, community involvement, financial need, hobbies, affiliations, personal characteristics, and special talents. Scholarships that are not based on financial need are usually called *merit-based* or *non-need scholarships*.
- A *grant* is also financial aid that does not have to be repaid. The most popular grants are the Pell Grant, the Student Incentive Grant, and the Supplemental Educational Opportunity Grant, all of which are awarded by the federal government and issued through academic institutions. All government grants are based primarily on need. However, there are many other grants that, like scholarships, are awarded for a variety of reasons.
- An *award* is also financial aid that does not have to be repaid.
- A *loan* is the only form of financial aid that you must repay, although some scholarships or grants may require you to work for a few years after you graduate as a type of repayment.
- A *fellowship* is an endowment to support individuals who want to obtain a graduate or doctoral degree.

THE LIBRARY

The library can be the most important source for a potential scholarship winner. Not only is it a quiet and comfortable place to concentrate, it also has vast information that is vital to your scholarship search. In addition, the library has friendly librarians who will be more than happy to help you find any information you require. It will save you time if you talk to them first about where to find information on various scholarships and other types of monetary aid. These materials are usually in one central area at the library. The sources you should look for are books, catalogs, directories, pamphlets, and brochures on scholarships. In these guides will be numerous college profiles listing basic facts about colleges and universities: campus acreage, number of students enrolled, year established, majors with the highest enrollment, special activities, percentage of financial need met, location, minority enrollment, and many other features. Information on various organizations can also be found, such as addresses, telephone numbers, types of scholarships and monetary awards, and application requirements. You will find material on government programs too.

If the library does not have the information you are seeking or does not have a large quantity of material on scholarships and financial aid, ask when it may have books on the subject in the near future. The librarian should be able to help you. Or you can visit your local bookstore. One book you may wish to look for that has a comprehensive list of scholarship program addresses is *The Scholarship Book* by Daniel J. Cassidy. If you cannot find this book, it can be ordered from your bookstore or the publisher; see Appendix B for the address.

THE RESEARCH QUESTIONNAIRE

The questions that follow will help narrow your particular attributes to correspond with the information you find at the library. They can pinpoint some special areas that you should look into for potential college dollars. For example, certain colleges and universities give scholarships to the children of their alumni. Likewise, some churches, fraternities, and other organizations give scholarships and monetary aid to children of their members.

These questions are also necessary because some books are only for minorities. Others deal specifically with children or close relatives of war veterans. There are also books covering scholarships for unusual hobbies or specific areas of interest; others are directed specifically toward women.

1. Where would you like to attend college? In what region? In what state?

- Look in guides and directories to find the colleges or universities that you list in response to this question. Look in regional guides such as *Peterson's Guide to Colleges in the Southeast* to find schools in the region and the state that you favor.

2. Would you settle for a college other than one of your initial choices if it offers you a scholarship and if its credentials are just as good?
    - If you answer yes to this question, you should look at all college profiles, regardless of location, in books such as *Peterson's Guide to Four-Year Colleges* or *Peterson's Guide to Two-Year Colleges* for schools that meet 100 percent of financial need. You should also look for colleges that have large scholarship programs.

3. What are your hobbies?
    - There are many scholarships for people who have particular hobbies. Books with extensive scholarship listings will have special sections dealing with these types of scholarships. Look for these special sections during your scholarship search.

4. For what company do you currently work?
    - Contact the personnel office of your employer to inquire about scholarship opportunities. If your company does not have a personnel office, speak with the general manager about the possibility of scholarship opportunities. Or contact the company's general headquarters to learn if such opportunities exist.

5. For what company or companies do your parents currently work?
    - Ask your parents to contact their personnel offices to inquire if there are scholarships available to the children of employees. If the locations of their respective jobs do not have personnel offices, they should speak with the general managers about the possibility of scholarship opportunities. Or contact the companies' general headquarters.

6. What is the denomination of the church you attend?
   • Many churches give scholarships not only to members of their congregations but to non-members as well. Some of them stipulate that the recipients of their scholarships must attend a college or university established to operate under the edicts of their denominational faith, such as a Presbyterian college or university. Contact churches and religious organizations to inquire about scholarships such as these. In addition, speak with the minister of the church that either you and/or your parents attend. Most churches are more than willing to establish a small scholarship fund for their students.

7. Are you a child or close relative of a war veteran? If so, in which war and in what branch of service did your relative serve?
   • Numerous scholarships are available for children and close relatives of veterans who served in specific wars, such as World War II. Books with extensive scholarship listings will have special sections dealing with these types of scholarships. Look for these special sections. You may need to know the branch in which your relative served.

8. Are you a disabled veteran?
   • Scholarship and financial assistance is available to most disabled veterans. Especially available is aid from the government. If you are a disabled veteran, contact the Federal Student Aid Information Center (800-433-3243) to inquire about scholarship opportunities. In addition, while researching scholarships, look for books that have sections compiled specifically for disabled veterans.

9. Are you legally blind, or do you have any other disabilities?
   • Students who are legally blind or in some other way disabled can usually receive scholarships and financial aid assistance from many sources, especially the government. During your search, look for directories that have special sections dealing with scholarships in this area.

10. Are you a member of a minority? If so, to what ethnic group do you belong?
    • There are numerous minority scholarships. Most scholarship directories have sections listing scholarship opportunities for minorities. During your search you may also find books that deal exclusively with scholarship opportunities for minorities.
11. For minority groups other than African-American, can you trace your lineage? (For example, Samoan, Japanese, Native American, etc.)
    • Many programs have scholarships strictly for minorities of a certain descent. To win these scholarships you are usually required to prove your lineage. Make sure to look for scholarships such as these if you fall into this category.
13. What are you strongly interested in studying at college?
    • Scholarships are available to students interested in a particular major. If you are certain of your intended major, look for directories and scholarship opportunities in the area in which you are interested.
14. Are you a member of a fraternity or sorority?
    • Most sororities and fraternities sponsor scholarships. As you look through scholarship directories, look for scholarships sponsored by your fraternity or sorority. If you are unable to discover any, write to the national chapter of your organization.
15. Are your parents members of a fraternity or sorority?
    • Some sororities and fraternities sponsor scholarships for the children of their members. As you look through scholarship directories, look for scholarships sponsored by your parents' fraternity or sorority. If you are unable to discover any, write to the national chapters of their organizations.
16. Are your parents alumni of a college or university?
    • Many colleges and universities offer scholarships to the children of their alumni. Contact the college or univer-

sity they attended to inquire about scholarship opportunities that may be available to you.

The books that you should find on scholarships, grants, and other types of monetary aid usually list in alphabetical order the names of various programs, their addresses, telephone numbers, special requirements, and deadlines. As you look through these books deciding which programs apply to you, you should begin recording names, addresses, telephone numbers, and deadlines.

Research Checklist

1. Be certain you understand and remember the key terms and facts explained in the beginning of the chapter.
2. Have you conducted your research in the library? Refer to Appendix B for specific titles to seek out.
3. Did you look for catalogs, books, directories, pamphlets, brochures, guides?
4. Have you pinpointed the special areas outlined in the Research Questionnaire?

INFORMATION ON COLLEGES

In addition to collecting books about scholarships and monetary aid, gather books on colleges and universities in general. When you look through these you will find common facts on colleges as well as information on financial aid. Colleges that boast 100 percent of financial need met usually have huge scholarship programs. After reading the preliminary information about the institutions you think you may be interested in attending, record the addresses of those colleges. A sample college profile with preliminary information contains the following:

• *General information* provides a brief overview of the college. It describes the type of institution it is, such as a four-year or two-year institution. It also gives the location and the date it was founded.

- *The academic information* section describes academic components of the college, including the faculty-to-student ratio, the number of volumes the library contains, and majors with the highest enrollment.
- *Statistics of the student body* contains such information as the number of minorities and transfer students enrolled.
- *Expenses* categorizes the costs associated with attending the college. For example, tuition and room and board are listed separately.
- *The financial aid* section deals with the amount of financial aid the college offers the average student and the percentage of financial need that is met by the college.
- *Admissions information* gives details about the application process and lists documents required for acceptance consideration.
- *Transfer admissions* outlines the requirements for a transfer student to be admitted to the college.
- *Entrance difficulty* describes the difficulty involved in gaining admittance to the college.
- *Further information* gives the address, name, and title of a person you can contact for more information about the college and the programs it offers.

It is important that you read the beginning, explanatory chapters of the directory, guide, or book to help you to completely understand how the information inside is organized.

If the library in your hometown keeps pamphlets and brochures in its vertical files, scan them. They may have information on scholarship programs or colleges that have large financial aid programs. Before you leave the library, or after repeated visits, take the time to catalog your information in some specific order. It saves time later, especially if you do it according to deadlines. Chapter 2, "Getting Organized," will contain more information about cataloging and how to keep track of all the material you have gathered.

The next step in the scholarship search process is the local telephone book. Use it to locate and record the addresses of all the major businesses in your area. Some companies may fund scholarships of which the general public may not be aware. Also, look for clubs, sororities, and fraternities, on local and national levels, because they usually offer scholarships. You should find the address for the Chamber of Commerce, too, if there is one in your area. The Chamber of Commerce may have knowledge of scholarships sponsored by businesses in your area.

The organizations listed below may or may not sponsor awards in your area, but this is a starting point and it should lead you in the right direction.

List of Sponsoring Organizations

American Bar Association
American Foundation for Pharmaceutical Education
American Heart Association
American Home Economics Association
American Institute of Architects Foundation
American Institute of Certified Public Accountants
American Legion
American Political Science Association
American Red Cross
American Society of Civil Engineers
American Society for Engineering Education
American Society of Military Comptrollers
Armstrong World Industries
Boy Scouts/Girl Scouts of America
Chamber of Commerce
Coca-Cola Scholars Foundation
Daughters of the American Revolution
Daughters of the Confederacy
Elks Club
4-H Club
Jaycees
Jostens

Kiwanis International
Knights of Columbus
Lions Club
Masons
National Association for the Advancement of Colored People
National Exchange Clubs
National Honor Society
National Scholarship Trust Fund
Optimist International
PepsiCo
Presbyterian Church
Rotary Club
Service Merchandise
Soroptimist International
Wal-Mart Stores
Westinghouse Electric Corporation
YMCA/YWCA

Write to the trust departments of all your local banks. Sometimes banks and other financial institutions have trusts set up by patrons to administer scholarships to deserving students who meet specific qualifications. The same may be true of radio and television stations in your area. They may advertise scholarship programs and would thus be able to supply you with information about them. In addition, write to your local Board of Education and inquire about special scholarships for high school graduates who would like to become teachers. There are scholarships of this type in many areas.

The next step is drafting two business letters, one that applies only to colleges and another that applies only to independent organizations sponsoring scholarships. (Independent scholarships can be used at any institution subject to the sponsor's requirements, while college-sponsored scholarships are for that institution only.) Avoid misspelled names, incorrect titles, and incomplete addresses by calling organizations to ensure the accuracy of your information.

Sample College/University Letter

500 Scholarship Street
Opportunity, Georgia 00000

December 16, 1993

Name of Admissions Director
Director of Admissions
The name of the college you are writing to
City, State, Zip Code

Dear *Name of Admissions Director:*

The time is rapidly approaching for me to choose a college. I am interested in *Anytown College* as a possible choice. Therefore, I would like to request a catalog and applications for admission and financial aid to help me become more familiar with *Anytown College* and the requirements needed to apply. I am also interested in reviewing any brochures about your institution, especially those relating to *internships, preprofessional programs, and financial aid.* I appreciate your assistance.

Sincerely yours,
Your signature
Your name, typed

---

* Note: Items in italics denote elements that should be changed to suit your specific letter.

Sample Private Scholarship Inquiry Letter
(This letter can be used for banks, churches, sororities, and other private organizations.)

500 Scholarship Street
Opportunity, Georgia 00000

December 16, 1993

National Scholarship Trust Fund
Graphic Arts Technical Foundation
4615 Forbes Avenue
Pittsburgh, Pennsylvania 15213

To whom it may concern:

I would like to receive more information about the scholarship(s) and/or award(s) listed in various resource materials. I would also like to receive an application as well as notification of special guidelines, deadlines, or other pertinent information, if any. Please send this information as soon as possible. If you need any further information from me, my number is *(912) 555-1111*.

Thank you for your assistance,
Your signature
Your name, typed

Sending letters to organizations and colleges and universities is a very important step in your scholarship search. The information you request and subsequently receive is essential to the success of your scholarship search for two crucial reasons: 1) It lists the requirements governing the scholarship or financial aid; and 2) it includes applications. The listing of requirements helps you to determine whether you are eligible to apply and also

---

° Note: Items in italics denote elements that should be changed to suit your specific letter.

helps you to determine whether you will apply for the scholarship. In all cases you should have a positive attitude and apply. However, you should be wary of scholarship programs that specifically state their scholarships are only for students interested in a certain area, such as engineering or graphic arts. If you are unsure of your intended major, then applying for a scholarship of this type may not be wise. In addition to sending applications and stating requirements, most colleges and universities usually include brochures concerned with meeting the costs of attending in their correspondence. These brochures list programs that are financially responsive to the needs of prospective students.

Once you have prepared your letters, you should mail them to every address on your list. Ideally you should mail them simultaneously, because it is easier to keep track of responses. Make a note of the date you send them out. For some organizations you may have to follow up your letter with a phone call or another letter if they do not respond to your initial letter within six weeks. Also, send a letter to the Department of Education, Publications Division, 400 Maryland Avenue, SW, Washington, D.C. 20202, for information on all federally funded programs. Many scholarship services charge $25, $35, even as much as $200 to uncover scholarship sources that can be found at this address free of charge. Some services that guarantee to locate at least six or eight scholarship sources merely send addresses gleaned from the Department of Education. If you decide to use a scholarship service, to get the most for your money you should try to find out as much as you can about the service by consulting the Better Business Bureau.

Important Questions to Ask Scholarship Services

1. How often do you update your database?
2. What is the success rate for students who utilize your services?
3. How long will it take you to send a listing to me?

4. Will the listing be sent in time for me to meet the deadlines of the scholarships and programs?
5. What percentage of your information is composed of well-known, federally funded programs such as the Pell Grant?
6. Will your list contain loans as scholarship sources?
7. Will your list be tailored to fit me? For example, if I am an international student, will the list contain addresses of programs that are only for U.S. citizens?

If you decide to use a computerized scholarship search, send your personal information in very early, ideally in the fall of your junior year. Often these services send information late, so avoid that problem by contacting them as early as possible. If you are a senior in high school and are looking for scholarship information it may be too late for you to use a computerized scholarship search and your money could be wasted. It may take more energy but I think you can do an excellent job on your own to find scholarship sources without having to pay. However, there are a few reputable services that can be relied upon for accurate and timely information, even if you should happen to be a high school senior, an undergraduate, or a graduate student. If you decide to use a computerized scholarship search service, I recommend the National Scholarship Research Service. For more information, write to: 2280 Airport Boulevard, Santa Rosa, California 95403 or call 1-800-432-3782. For information on Peterson's computerized financial aid listing service, call 1-800-EDU-DATA. Other scholarship research services can be found be in the Yellow Pages of your local telephone book under the heading EDUCATIONAL CONSULTANTS.

COLLEGE FAIRS

To gather additional information, attend college fairs where representatives from over three hundred colleges and universities distribute information and talk to prospective students and their parents. Attending these fairs will also help you get a feel for a college or university by talking to student or faculty representatives. If your intention is to enroll in a popular university, the number of people visiting each booth will answer that question. The fairs (also called "college probe fairs") are held in most major cities across the nation during the course of a year, and they usually begin in September. Contact your guidance counselor about dates and locations. Most of the college fairs are conducted in shopping malls, so you can call the events coordinator in the mall or malls for the dates of future college fairs in your area.

Questions You Should Ask at College Fairs

1. What percentage of students attending your college receives scholarships and financial aid?
2. What percentage of the scholarships is based on financial need?
3. What percentage of the scholarships is based on merit?
4. What is the name of the financial aid director?
5. Does the institution conduct a large scholarship competition? If so, how many levels are there?
6. What is the deadline for the application for admission?
7. What is the deadline for the application for financial aid and scholarships?

Materials You Should Ask for at College Fairs

1. College or university catalog.
2. Application for admission. Glance through it immediately to see if you have any questions.
3. Scholarship and financial aid applications.
4. Any other brochures or materials they have on the college or university.

CAMPUS VISITS

A campus visit is an effective method of obtaining an overall impression of a college or university. Many students have determined during a campus visit if they are truly interested in attending an institution. My campus visit certainly changed my mind. Before the recruiter from Florida A & M University contacted me, I really knew nothing about the school and had already decided to attend a university in New Orleans. I did not want to visit another school, simply because I had made my decision about where I was going to college and had no intention of changing my mind. However, after being convinced by my brother Dutch that I should visit, I went to the campus in July of 1991. Before I left, Florida A & M University had become my future alma mater.

As you can see, a campus visit is a very effective decision-making tool. It can give you a chance to absorb the academic atmosphere by talking with faculty members and students, walking around the campus, sitting in classes, eating in the dining halls, sleeping in the dormitories, and wandering around the surrounding city. Not only does a visit give *you* a chance to assess the college or university, it also gives university officials a chance to view you as a prospective student. Throughout campus visits you are given chances to ask questions about the curriculum, possible majors, and academic resources, such as computer availability and library hours. You can also ask students about the social and extracurricular activities at the college.

Arranging a campus visit is usually done through the admissions office. One-day or overnight visits are available. If possible, you should plan to make your visit when the school is in regular session; for example, in the fall or spring. This way you can be assured of getting a realistic view of the college at a time when you will most likely be there if you should decide to attend. Most colleges will plan activities for student visitors and will allow you to attend classes. Remember, if it is a weekend designated for prospective students to visit, you are likely to see the most positive aspects of the school. While these types of visits are very informative and lots of fun, try to arrange another visit so that you can see what the institution is *really* like.

Research Checklist

1. Have you exhausted the resources of the public library? For example, have you looked in all scholarship directories, vertical files of pamphlets and brochures, magazines, books, college catalogs?
2. Have you looked in general college guides such as *Peterson's Guide to Colleges in the Southeast*?
3. Have you looked in the telephone book for local private organizations such as fraternities, sororities, and clubs?
4. Have you contacted national associations and clubs?
5. Have you contacted the local radio station?
6. Have you contacted the Chamber of Commerce in your area?
7. Have you talked with your guidance counselor about college fairs in your area, or attended one?
8. Have you visited a nearby college campus?
9. Have you contacted the banks in your area about trust funds?
10. Have you contacted the Board of Education and asked about special scholarships for students who would like to become teachers?

Throughout your journey on the road to winning scholarships you must be alert to any information that can be used to find scholarship dollars. For example, while listening to the radio, watching television, reading, and talking to people, you may become aware of new scholarship opportunities.

*I should never have made my success in life
if I had not bestowed upon the least thing I have
ever undertaken, the same attention and care
that I have bestowed upon the greatest.*

—————————

Charles Dickens

◆

2

GETTING ORGANIZED

$\mathcal{D}$o you have enough information to fill an entire table and all of its chairs? I hope you do, because I did. (I had so much material that my mother had given up the idea of cleaning the room I occupied!) At this point you should have numerous catalogs, brochures, pamphlets, and applications, not only for the colleges that you are interested in but for many that you are not. You should also have numerous scholarship applications for private organizations. If you don't, you soon will—if you followed the instructions in Chapter 1. When almost every available surface in your scholarship-planning room is covered with material, it's time to go forward and organize. Read this chapter carefully to avoid missing out on opportunities simply because you've lost sight of an application that may be hiding under the edge of a book. If you are not organized it may stay hidden just until the deadline has passed. Since that is definitely not what you want to happen, let's get organized.

Prepare file folders for each organization or college and put all relative information into its corresponding file. If you have an available file cabinet, organize all the files according to deadline dates. If you do not have a file cabinet, a box will serve the purpose just as well. On each file folder write the deadline date in large, eye-catching letters so that you can see them as you flip through your file cabinet or box.

As you organize your information and put it into files, there should not be anything that you have not read. It is essential to read everything sent to you. There are many opportunities that you can miss if you do not take the time to carefully read all the information sent in correspondence packages. This is especially true for packages sent by college recruiters.

About one third of the letters sent to you by independently sponsored organizations may contain notices stating they are out of funds, or their scholarships are only for the children of their employees, or you are not in the specific region that they are trying to reach. These special requirements should have been listed in the scholarship books at the time of your initial research. Unfortunately, this information is rarely included. There are some programs that may ask for an application request in writing, or they may require you to go through other channels to obtain their application. Nevertheless, most programs send everything requested in the inquiry letter, including an application. Once you have received all the replies, favorable or not, again, read everything from top to bottom.

Purchase a calendar, or be enterprising and make one large enough to record information under the dates. Some applications require special information, but most require the same. If you keep certain facts about yourself and your family members handy (refer to Chapters 1 and 6)—for example, in the inside cover of your calendar—it will take less time to complete an application. Also in the inside cover of your calendar you should have deadlines posted, with reminder notes a week before the deadlines. In your calendar you should mark special dates at least three weeks before a deadline for requesting a recommendation and for giving those you request one from your personal résumé (explained in Chapter 5). When you give them your résumé you should include a self-addressed envelope with two stamps on it. You should also have checkpoint dates each week afterward, to remind them of their responsibility to you.

Make a recommendation list for future reference. Most applications require recommendations from at least three sources. In your repertoire make sure you include your high school's supervising principal or another key administrator, an English teacher, an employer (if you have one), and your minister. I recommend English teachers because they have usually mastered the art of writing recommendations for their students; but any teacher will do. You should also have at least ten others on the list who will write recommendations for you, to achieve variety and avoid tiring the main contributors on your list. You should make certain to include a few neighbors and friends, because some select programs may ask for recommendations from them. To make this easier you should draft a version of a recommendation letter stressing key points about your character for your friends and neighbors to use as a reference.

The sample list to follow will give you an idea of how to make a recommendations list for yourself. With a chart you can easily see whom you may need to write a particular type of recommendation. For example, referring to the chart, if you need a recommendation that emphasizes your leadership ability, you would want to approach Mr. B. Gooden, who knows of your skills from the time you spent as captain of the team for which he was an advisor. If you need one that emphasizes your position as an outstanding member of your high school community, then you would contact Ms. S. Samson. This chart should also keep you informed of who has written recommendations for you in the past and who is currently preparing one.

In addition to preparing background information and a recommendations reference list, you may need to take some pictures if you do not already have recent ones. Many scholarship programs like to see smiling faces in black and white two-by-three-inch photographs. These are usually for publicity purposes; in certain scholarship competitions a recent photograph will be requested.

Sample Recommendations Chart

Name of the person	Have they done a recommendation for me before?	Are they doing a recommendation for me now? When is it due?	How does this person know of me?
Mrs. A. Brown	No	No	Neighbor. She is a retired English teacher.
Mr. B. Gooden	Yes	No	Advisor of Science Bowl team. I have been the captain of the team for two years.
Ms. S. Samson	Yes	Yes. Due on 2/28/93	Principal of my high school.
Mrs. F. Champion	Yes	No	Red Cross youth coordinator. I have been a volunteer for four years.

SELECTING A COLLEGE THAT SUITS YOUR NEEDS

Prepare a preliminary list of college and universities you might be interested in attending. Make columns for characteristics you are looking for. The following exhibit is an excerpt from my preliminary list, to give you a working model.

I was particularly interested in universities or colleges that had cooperation programs with other schools where students could take classes. The first column, headed by *Co-op*, reflects that interest; the rows that have asterisks inside them had some cooperative class offerings but did not have a full program. I also wanted a college that had a large and beautifully landscaped campus, so I used acreage of the school as an indication. I also

Co-op	Acres	College/University	Telephone No.	Percent	Masters	Difficulty	ACT
Yes°	1200	Oakwood College	No listing	99	No	Easy	Yes
Yes	280	Samford College	No listing	5	Yes	Moderately	No
Yes	23	Xavier	No listing	94	Yes	Moderately	No
Yes°	168	Valdosta State	1-800-872-2586	14	Yes	Minimally	No
Yes°	1000	University of North Florida	No listing	7	Yes	Very	No

recorded the toll-free (1-800) telephone numbers that I found to request additional information by phone. I wanted to know the total minority enrollment, hence the percentages. The column entitled *Difficulty* refers to the difficulty in being admitted as a first-time student. The column entitled *ACT* pertains to colleges who accepted scores from the American College Test in place of SAT scores.

You can tailor your own chart to fit your interests. For instance, if your are interested in sports programs or literary associations on campus, you should have a checklist column for that. You could be interested in the faculty-to-student ratio, or the size of the community where the college is located. Your parents may also be interested in the community's crime rate. These are only a few of the areas that you can target in a school. This chart will help you find a college that would be best suited to you and your needs and also satisfy the concerns of your family.

Devise an overall monthly scholarship plan. This plan will help you see quickly the tasks you need to accomplish each month. I have included my five-month scholarship plan here for your reference.

Five-Month Plan
January 1–May 31

JANUARY

1. Fill out financial aid form. If I don't have my W-2, gather all other financial information needed to complete the application.
2. Fill out National Scholarship Trust Fund application.
3. Call C&S Bank about Jacques Foundation scholarship.
4. Write to NAACP for scholarship application.
5. Complete University of Georgia scholarship application:
   • Essay required
   • Need two recommendations, one from teacher and one from principal
6. Complete Rhodes College application:
   • Essay completed
7. Finish Georgia College application.
8. Fill out University of Alabama application.
9. Fill out Zeta Phi Beta scholarship application.

FEBRUARY

1. Finish Centre College application:
   • Essay needed
   • Recommendations needed
2. Furman University deadline:
   • Need essay
   • Need recommendations
3. Oglethorpe University application deadline.

MARCH

1. Complete application for Wesleyan College:
   • Essay required
   • Recommendation required
2. Finish Wendy's scholarship application.
3. Find War Memorial scholarship application.
4. Complete National Negro Business and Professional Women's Club's scholarship application.

APRIL

1. Winthrop College application needs the following:
   • Essay
   • Recommendation
2. Finish Herbert Lehman scholarship application.

MAY

Rest!!!

I also had a plan for the months immediately after my senior year of school began, September 1–December 31. Many of my scholarship deadlines fell during these months. Keep in mind that I made the January through May plan during the month of December and much of my work was done before I was actually required to complete and mail the applications. I kept notes and made plans like those previously mentioned, primarily as a reminder of recommendations I needed to check on and essays I needed to revise. Some of the organizations and institutions in the plan I decided not to apply to, because by the middle of April my future was set.

A scholarship plan for the months of September 1–December 31 should look like the example below. Deadlines for turning in materials will be different for various scholarships. Therefore, your plan may look very different from this example or the example before it. However, the months beginning your scholarship search should closely parallel the following example.

Four-Month Plan
September 1–December 31

SEPTEMBER

1. Go to library and conduct research. Gather addresses.
2. Draft two letters. Prepare one for colleges. Prepare one for private organizations.

3. Send letters.
4. Call or write local organizations and Chamber of Commerce.
5. Talk to counselor.
6. Register for the SAT and the ACT.

OCTOBER

1. Organize all replies that I have received thus far. Create reference files.
2. Prepare résumé.
3. Prepare two basic essays describing myself and my future career goals.
4. Make a recommendations list of teachers, friends, and employers.

NOVEMBER

Visit colleges.

DECEMBER

1. Make sure I have read all applications and materials sent by colleges and private organizations.
2. Be prepared to meet all deadlines.

The most integral contribution to my scholarship success was organization and preparation. Therefore, all the addresses and telephone numbers that are given in this book should be written to at once and used immediately to find out more information. It does not matter if you are a middle school or high school student, you should begin your preparation as soon as possible. Prior knowledge is the key to improved preparation and eventual success. However, if you are not a senior, the information you receive should be kept up-to-date by calling or writing the organization or institution each year until you are.

Nothing great was ever achieved without enthusiasm.

_____

Ralph Waldo Emerson

◆

3

GETTING THE MOST
FROM YOUR COUNSELOR

*I*f you are serious about pursuing a college career, any counselor who truly cares will try to help you. However, many of them
are swamped with the day-to-day details of registering students
for classes or various other activities, so they don't have time to
come to you with scholarship opportunities. You must make a
special effort to get to know your counselor. Make an appoint-
ment with him or her and discuss your hopes for the future and
your need for scholarship money. Talk over your academic
strengths and weaknesses. When you draft your résumé, make
sure your counselor is the first to get one, even if you don't need a
recommendation yet. Stay in close contact with your counselor
by visiting his or her office every day to learn about various
colleges and scholarship opportunities that may cross his or her
desk. Let the counselor know you are willing to apply for all
scholarships for which you are qualified.

Many times scholarship programs inform the counselors of
opportunities and request names of students who would be
interested in applying for a particular scholarship. Some programs will consider an applicant on the basis of a recommendation from the counselor only. Therefore, you should make sure
your counselor always has your name on his or her list of qualified and interested students.

In your senior year, make sure the counselor has your final

transcript prepared and ready to go at a moment's notice. Some high schools have a list in the office of the registrar for students to place the names of colleges and programs to which they need their final transcripts sent. Many colleges and universities will not allow you to register for classes if they have not received your final transcript. Likewise, some scholarship programs may disqualify your application if they do not have your transcript or a copy of your grades.

Information about scholarships, grants, and monetary aid should be in abundance at your household by now, so you should not need a counselor for that. However, just to make sure all the bases are covered, ask your counselor for additional information anyway. Often counselors hand out regenerated information from the Department of Education, whose address is given in Chapter 1, but they may have information neither I nor you have discovered.

Counselors usually have financial aid forms (FAFs) in their possession. Obtain one and start gathering the information the form requires as soon as possible, even though it cannot be completed and mailed until after January 1 of the year you plan to enter college. Most colleges require an FAF for scholarship consideration, even for merit-based scholarships.

The following checklist should help you gather the information you need for the financial aid application.

WHAT YOU NEED TO KNOW BEFORE
FILLING OUT THE FINANCIAL AID APPLICATION

- The total of all Social Security income received during the year for you and your parents
- The total of all Aid to Families with Dependent Children (AFDC) benefits for you and your parents
- The total of all child-support payments received in your household during the year

- The total of all other untaxed income and benefits during the year for you and your parents
- Current year's medical and dental expenses not paid by insurance for you and your parents
- Current year's elementary, junior high, and high school tuition paid by your parents
- Amount in cash, savings, and checking accounts for you and your parents
- Value of your home, or your parents', unless it's rented
- The purchase price paid for your home or your parents'
- The amount owed on your home or your parents'
- Value of all real estate and investments for yourself and your parents
- Value of all business and farm assets for yourself and your parents
- The total amount of veterans' benefits received during the current year, if any
- Expected income for you and your parents to be received in the following year

If you need a recommendation from your counselor, you should give him or her at least two months' advance notice, if possible; include a copy of your résumé, and a stamped and self-addressed envelope. Remember to have a checkpoint date for them as well.

Almost all scholarship applications need a counselor's signature, and they may need other information that only your counselor or registrar has access to, such as class size, your class ranking, grade point average, and the exact number of credits you have earned. Since counselors are responsible for many tasks in a high school, give them a little time to get this information. Make sure you continually check with them to see if they have completed what you have given them. Once you have fully completed all of the information required for an application, put everything in the envelope, affix the proper postage, address the envelope, make sure you include your return address, and give it to your counselor. Tell him or her it needs to be mailed immediately. Make sure your application is mailed in adequate time to reach its deadline. In addition to making the deadlines, some scholarships are based on a first-come, first-served basis. Therefore, you should go to your counselor's office often to ensure that your application will be received well ahead of its deadline.

All common things, each day's events,
that with the hour begin and end,
our pleasures and our discontents
are rounds by which we may ascend.

———————

Henry Wadsworth Longfellow

◆

4

TAKING TESTS

*7*he Scholastic Aptitude Test (SAT) is a necessity for most scholarship programs, especially those administered by colleges. The SAT is a three-hour, multiple-choice exam composed of six segments that measure mathematical and verbal abilities. The six segments consist of two thirty-minute sections that test your vocabulary, verbal reasoning, and reading comprehension. There are also two thirty-minute sections that test your mathematical skills in the areas of arithmetic, geometry, and algebra. These segments comprise the sections of the test that are scored. The remaining sections are the Test of Standard Written English (TSWE), and an experimental section that, depending upon the exam version, may be another verbal, mathematical, or TSWE section.

Taking the SAT is a free booklet given at the time of registration for the SAT. Registration for the SAT or the ACT (American College Test) usually occurs about six to eight weeks before the date of the exam. *Taking the SAT* gives details about the test. It also contains sample questions and a practice test from a previously used SAT complete with the answers and explanations. Read this booklet very carefully. See if you can get copies of the booklet from previous years as well, so that you can take more than one of the sample tests.

Many students do not take the time to read these booklets and often miss out on important facts, especially if it is the first time they are taking the test. For example, points are deducted for wrong answers, so those who randomly guess at answers may be actually lowering their scores considerably; also, questions at the beginning of the tests are much easier than those at the end. These booklets show you how the tests are scored, and the practice test gives you a chance to score your own.

Take the practice test in the booklet under conditions that will be similar to the actual testing situation. Set up a room with a clear desk or small table and declare it off-limits to other family members. All noise should be kept to a minimum. Take the test using a sharpened No. 2 pencil; have an extra nearby. If possible, take the test in the morning beginning at 9:00 o'clock. Have someone monitor the time. If you run out of time while attempting to complete a section, do not finish it. Go on to the next section, as you will be expected to do on the day of the actual test. After you have finished the practice test, go over your incorrect responses and the correct solutions and their explanations carefully. Finish the questions you did not have time for and then look at the solutions for those. Try to establish a pattern in the questions you habitually miss. If you do find a pattern, there may be a concept or word that you do not fully understand that causes you to select the incorrect answer.

In addition to the SAT, the ACT should be taken as well. It is permissible and highly recommended that you take both of them as soon as possible. Both tests have preliminary versions, the PSAT and the PACT, explained later in this chapter. If you wish, you can start by taking those to warm up for the actual test. In my opinion the preliminary versions are somewhat harder than the actual SAT or ACT tests. Therefore, if you practice with those you will have a very good background, especially if you take them first in middle school.

There is a program in some if not all parts of the United States called the Educational Talent Search. Through this program the SAT is administered to seventh- and eighth-grade students. Those who score in an acceptable range are given scholarships to Duke University, a private institution in Durham, North Carolina. If you would like more information about the program or you want to know the exact qualifications, write to Duke University or the College Board Educational Talent Search Program. Both addresses are listed in Appendix A.

In addition to the Educational Talent Search Program, the Preliminary Scholastic Aptitude Test (PSAT), taken in the tenth grade, is also a qualifying test for the National Merit/Achievement Scholarship Competition (officially named Preliminary Scholastic Aptitude Test/National Merit Scholarship Qualifying Test—PSAT/NMSQT). Again, scoring in a certain range reaps great rewards. If you score high on this test it will place you in a large national competition that goes through several different levels. Students who become finalists in this competition are eligible for many scholarship opportunities from corporations and institutions. When you register for the PSAT you will receive *The Student Bulletin*. In addition to test-taking tips, sample questions, and a practice test, it contains extensive information about the PSAT as a qualifying test for two scholarship programs, the National Merit Scholarship Program and the National Achievement Scholarship Program for Outstanding Negro Students. For more information about these programs, contact the National Merit Scholarship Corporation (PSAT/NMSQT), One Rotary Center, 1560 Sherman Avenue, Evanston, IL 60201; (708) 866-5100. In order to take advantage of the opportunities that scholarships like these provide, it would be very beneficial to begin familiarizing yourself with standardized tests as soon as possible.

Do not feel that if you have progressed beyond the seventh, eighth, or tenth grade and have not taken these tests that all hope is lost. I personally did not start my scholarship search until the beginning of my senior year. However, I laid the preliminary groundwork for it years earlier, as I had already been involved in various extracurricular activities and had taken the SAT twice. It helps if you take the SAT as many times as you can afford the extra expense. They do have fee waivers for those who cannot afford to pay the full price, which is $19 for the SAT and $22 for the ACT. Call the Educational Testing Service (ETS) at (609) 683-0441 for current information. Since the tests are timed, it will eventually improve your score if you become more familiar with the formats of both the SAT and the ACT.

SAT and ACT scores can vary for a number of reasons. Many students are not good test takers in any situation. Others are plagued by anxiety attacks. Some may not have had enough sleep the night before the test. The testing environment may be poor. Many factors can contribute to a low test score other than lack of knowledge. Scholarship programs and colleges take these factors into account. In fact, Harvard Business School does not require, accept, or consider scores from the GMAT, the standardized test for entrance to a graduate school of management. Therefore, most programs concentrate on the well-rounded student who is active in his or her high school and community. If you exhibit excellent qualities in other areas, your test-taking skills or lack of them will not hold you back. This is not to say that improving test scores is not important. What it does say is that a student who has excellent grades, excellent test scores, and is also involved in a variety of extracurricular activities has an even better chance for taking advantage of scholarship opportunities.

When you receive your test scores, carefully note weak areas which will be centered in either the verbal court or the mathematical court. There are various books in the library and the bookstores for improving test scores in either area or both, but I suggest that you reread the booklet *Taking the SAT*.

My personal suggestion for improving verbal scores is to read as much as possible. Extensive reading helps increase your vocabulary as well as your word usage. Effective reading skills can improve your ability to understand situations, make accurate evaluations, and compare ideas, which are skills needed for the verbal portions of the SAT and the ACT.

Another way to improve your vocabulary is to learn the meanings of as many prefixes, suffixes, and roots of the English language as you can. Courses in Latin can be very helpful in this area. If you have a good understanding of the English language and its origins, you will be able to easily grasp and understand the meanings of words that you have never seen before. For example, the prefix *mono-* means "single" or "one." Therefore, the following words preceded by *mono-* have definitions that all include the words *single* or *one*. These words and definitions have been extracted from *Webster's New World Dictionary*.

monodrama: a drama acted or written to be performed by *one* person

monody: in ancient Greek literature, an ode sung by a *single* voice

monomerous: having *one* member

monogamy: the practice or state of being married to only *one* person at a time

monomania: an excessive interest in or enthusiasm for *one* thing

monocle: an eyeglass for *one* eye only

Always keep a dictionary and a thesaurus handy to look up unfamiliar words when you are reading. This will help you become accustomed to using and comprehending a variety of words.

The ACT measures your knowledge of math, English, reading, and science reasoning. After taking this test you should assess your weak areas. There are books in the library and in bookstores for improving ACT scores. Also, the registration packet for the ACT comes with a booklet and practice test that help students to become more familiar with the actual test format and questions.

The SAT and the ACT are excellent sources for information. When registering for the SAT, students who fill in the *yes* oval on the registration form that asks whether you would like to participate in the Student Search Service will receive free information about colleges and universities. They also receive information about scholarship programs sponsored by colleges and universities as well as the government. The information you provide on your registration form is transmitted to other scholarship programs that may be interested in you as one of their scholars;

this information includes place of residence, range of test scores (not your actual test scores—they do not give these out unless you request it), grade point average, intended college major, ethnic background, and religious preference. If the programs are interested they will send you information. When you receive it, read everything; most offer wonderful scholarship packages.

The registration forms for the SAT and the ACT will request that you list scholarship programs and institutions that you want to receive your scores. If you do not have them available at the time of your registration, then you will have another chance to make your request and any corrections when you reach the test site on the day of the test.

For most scholarships, college or private, you will need to take some type of standardized test. For U.S. citizens it is usually the SAT or the ACT. Foreign students will need to take the Test of English as a Foreign Language (TOEFL). Starting early and taking these tests as soon as possible, well before your senior year of high school, will boost your confidence and your scores.

*A successful man is one who has tried,
not cried; who has worked, not dodged;
who has shouldered responsibility, not evaded it;
who has gotten under the burden instead of
standing off, looking on and giving advice.*

Eliot Hubbard

◆

5

GRADES DON'T MEAN EVERYTHING

*F*or someone to invest, he or she must first have a reason to invest. In order for someone to invest in you, it is necessary to sell yourself through words and actions. In Chapter 7 we will deal with words. In this chapter we are concerned with actions in the form of your personal résumé.

Myth 1:
You must be an "A" student to win a scholarship.

Fact:
There are many students who do have "A" averages and have been unable to obtain scholarship funds. The Coca-Cola Scholars Foundation conducts one of the largest corporate-sponsored scholarship programs in the United States. As a student who participated in the 1991 Coca-Cola Scholars competition, I became aware of many recipients of the $4,000 and $20,000 scholarship awards who were not "A" students. Essentially, the winners were determined by factors such as community-based extracurricular activities. In fact, although a good academic record is a contributing factor, having an "A" average exclusively would not qualify a student as a Coca-Cola Scholar. Coca-Cola Scholars are well-rounded, unique, and independent individuals.

Myth 2:
A "B" or a "C" student cannot get a scholarship because he or she is just average.

Fact:
Students who have "B" and "C" averages can get scholarships, easily. The Coca-Cola Scholars Foundation is one example. The David Letterman Scholarship, aimed at individuals who do not have higher than a "C" average, is another. There are many scholarships that are not determined solely on the basis of grades. In fact, there are many sources of financial aid that are "grade blind," meaning that these programs do not recognize grades as a determining factor.

Myth 3:
Minorities and impoverished students get scholarships because they are underprivileged. The middle-class student is always left out.

Fact:
The majority of my scholarships were based on merit, which has no regard to race. I am a minority student but I am economically middle class. The government did not offer any assistance. Although there are many scholarships aimed at minorities, there are many that are based solely on individual merit. In a 1993 poll, statistics compiled by Denise M. Topolnicki for *Money* magazine showed that Tulane University, Emory University, Providence College, and Bard College were among the ten top schools who have the largest average merit-based scholarship programs. Myths 1, 2, and 3 are just that—myths. Grades do not make a well-rounded individual, and minorities and the poor do not get all the good scholarships.

Good grades play an important role in the scholarship process, yet they should not be used as an excuse not to apply for scholarships. Most scholarship programs look for well-rounded individuals who not only excel academically but are involved in extra-curricular activities as well. To them the perfect candidate would be one who has a perfect score on the SAT (1800), the ACT (36), and a 4.0 grade point average or higher, depending on the grading scale for honors classes. When I tell people that my grade point average was 4.67, they usually look at me with an expression of disbelief. A 4.67 was possible for me, as I'm sure it is for many of you, because honors classes at our high school were on a five-point scale system; a variety of honors courses, especially advanced-placement courses, can boost your grade point average above the usual perfect 4.0. In addition to perfect test scores and a perfect record in the classroom, colleges look for the ingredient that can label a student as a possessor of the "total package": extracurricular activities in school and the community. The student who has these qualities will not have a problem being accepted to any college he or she desires or in winning the money to pay for it. However, if the student I have just outlined describes you, self-motivation, determination, and persistence are still required, because unless you are an athlete who has received a lot of publicity, most schools will not come to you waving scholarship money. You still need to work hard.

EXTRACURRICULAR ACTIVITIES

Extracurricular activities tell scholarship program administrators that as a student you are willing to devote your time and effort to your community and school. By investing their scholarship dollars in you, they are not only investing in *your* future, they are investing in the future of the country. Therefore, it is necessary to participate in projects for your school and community, because these activities convey that you are a self-motivated leader with potential. Not only does involvement in extracurricular activities express your leadership qualities, it can build them as well. A list of these activities on your résumé is very impressive when you include it with your application.

Also, participation in contests and other activities related to your specific interests, such as piano or dance recitals, horse shows, and poetry or oratorical contests, can show another impressive side to you. Participation in various contests shows that you are not afraid of competition and creates an impression of a well-rounded and involved student. My special interest was writing. A condensed form of my résumé, Résumé A on page 50, shows mostly awards won in writing competitions. It is organized as follows: Departmental Clubs/Activities, with another heading for Honorary Clubs, and yet another heading for Community Clubs/Activities. Then I listed awards and honors under a separate heading beginning with the ninth grade. I prepared several variations of this basic résumé for different programs. One excerpt from a variation, shown in Résumé B on page 51, displays the amount of hours spent for each activity; still another lists each club or activity I was involved in; and under these are listed the awards I had won through each club or activity. All of these are merely examples to give you guidelines to follow. The way you organize your résumé may be according to your own personal involvement, style, and preference.

Going on school field trips to participate in seminars or workshops for educational or community-interest projects can also be included in your résumé as extracurricular activities. You can create a separate heading for special-interest activities. While reviewing my résumé you may wonder if it is necessary to be involved in so many activities. No, it is not necessary to be involved in as many clubs and activities as I was. It is very easy to stretch yourself too thin. I liked to be involved in everything, but you don't have to do that. One or two activities that you are really interested in is fine, especially if you have a position of leadership. If you are not a member of any club and don't participate in outside activities, I strongly suggest you become involved in some type of extracurricular activity. Participation of any type can help you grow and improve in many areas. One key area is interaction with others in a group setting, beyond the typical classroom environment. This shows your willingness to get involved in your surroundings and make a positive contribution. Also, in reference to winning awards for your activities, even if you have not received honors it looks good to participate. Repeated and improved participation shows that not only are you a good sport, you can learn from your mistakes.

Clubs and activities that are considered impressive are the Beta Club, Student Council, and the National Honor Society. It really doesn't matter what clubs or activities you become involved in, but these are nationally known for leadership, service, and involvement in the community. If you don't have any of these clubs at your high school, get in contact with a national or local representative and start one. Scholarship programs like to see students who initiate and carry out challenging ideas.

Either format, Résumé A or B, is fine. Some scholarship programs request your activities listed in a certain order, and you should comply with their rules. In most cases both forms are acceptable.

SAMPLE RÉSUMÉ A

Marianne Ragins (*Substitute your name and address.*)
Post Office Box 6845
Macon, Georgia 31208

Northeast Comprehensive High School (*Substitute your school name and address.*)
1646 Upper River Road
Macon, Georgia 31201

Departmental Clubs/Activities (*Here list all activities you are involved in within your school.*)
Academic Bowl Team: 9th–12th (*List activity and grades in which you participated.*)
 Captain: 11th (*List any positions of leadership held and the grade held as a subheading.*)
Drama Club: 9th–12th

Salmagundi Literary Magazine: 10th–12th
 Assistant Editor: 10th
 Co-Editor: 11th
 Editor in Chief: 12th
Student Council: 9th–12th
 President: 12th
Honorary Clubs (*List all clubs that you have been inducted into because of outstanding performance.*)
Mu Alpha Theta: 10th–12th
National Honor Society: 10th–12th
Community Clubs/Activities (*Clubs or activities within the community.*)
Macon Telegraph and News Teen Board: 1991 (*List the calendar year[s] involved.*)
Red Cross Youth Volunteer: 1988–1989
Y-Club: 1988–1991
 Vice President: 1989–1990
Awards/Honors (*List all the awards that you have won throughout high school. Include certificates of participation.*)
Best Poem in State—Georgia Scholastic Press Association
National English Merit Award
Certificate of Participation—Mathematics Meet, 1987

SAMPLE RÉSUMÉ B

Marianne Ragins (*Substitute your name and address.*)
Post Office Box 6845
Macon, Georgia 31208

Northeast Comprehensive High School (*Substitute your school name and address.*)
1646 Upper River Road
Macon, Georgia 31201

School Activities, Awards, and Honors
(*Here list all positions of leadership, number of hours spent in each activity, and awards won.*)
Academic Bowl Team Captain: 11th, 12th—15 hours/month
Macon Telegraph and News Teen Board Layout Editor: 12th—28 hours/month
Salmagundi Literary Magazine Assistant Editor: 10th—20 hours/month
    First Place—Georgia Scholastic Press Association, 1989 (*List awards won as a member of the organization.*)
    First Place—Columbia Scholastic Press Association, 1989

I wonder if the human touch which people have
is not one of the greatest assets that you can have. . . .
You read a book, sit before the performance
of a fine actor, or read a poem—and there it is—
something that streams into your consciousness . . .
without this human touch, hope has little
on which to feed or thrive.

———————

George Matthew Adams

◆

6

THE APPLICATION

*A*t this point in your scholarship journey everything should come together. Your extensive research has rewarded you with numerous applications. The organizational procedure in Chapter 2 has provided you with the knowledge to compartmentalize your applications and supporting documents. You have people such as your counselor and principal on your recommendations list. Your academic and extracurricular interests are clearly outlined. You have also taken or registered for the SAT and the ACT. In addition, your résumé, explained in Chapter 5, has been completed and will highlight your commitment to society, your school, and your personal improvement. You are now ready to apply for admission to college and for scholarships.

The most crucial stage of your quest for college scholarships will be completing applications, fees for which range from $10 to $60. The first item that college and scholarship administrators will see is your application. The first impression will be made through the application you submit. If your application is sloppy, they will get that impression of you before they have a chance to formulate positive assessments. This impression may cause them to scrap your entire application; then all your painstaking work on the essay, your résumé, and other supporting material will be wasted. So let's strive to have an application that is not only neat but free of errors and complete with required information.

Having followed the instructions provided in the previous chapters, this step should be easy for you.

If you cannot type well and you know that you are prone to make numerous mistakes that would result in an application littered with White-Out, ask a friend or family member to do it for you. If that is not feasible, hire someone or be extra conscientious.

Tip 1

All applications should be typed, no exceptions—unless the application requests that you print. If so, use black ink.

Tip 2

Make photocopies of applications as you receive them. To avoid mistakes, for your typist and yourself, fill out the photocopied applications well ahead of the deadline. Also, make a handwritten list for your typist and yourself of frequently asked questions and their answers. You will find a list of typical questions asked on applications at the end of this chapter. Always keep a copy of your completed applications. You may need them to prepare for interviews.

Tip 3

Set up a file system for all copies of applications so that you can locate them easily as deadlines draw near. A filing system is also helpful because you can refer to an application for information to use on another one.

Tip 4

All sections of the application that you are not directly responsible for should be given to those who are responsible for them as soon as possible. For example, recommendation forms for counselors, teachers, and friends, or secondary- and mid-year school reports.

Tip 5

Arrange to have your scores from the SAT, ACT, and other standardized tests sent to the colleges shortly after your applications arrive, if you have not already done so during the registration phase for the tests. Make sure to check with the colleges and universities to ensure that they have received them.

Tip 6
Have two-by-three-inch black-and-white photographs prepared with your name, address, and telephone number typed on the back. Only include a photo if asked.

Tip 7
Include your personal résumé. Most applications have space for you to list your activities and special awards, but it looks more professional to include a résumé. Never leave the spaces for this information blank. Instead, type instructions to see additional information on a separate sheet. The separate sheet will be your résumé.

Tip 8
Do not type essays or other supporting material on erasable bond typing paper. This is not professional and can be messy.

Tip 9
Some programs that issue applications specifically request that additional pages be kept to a minimum if they are allowed at all. Respect their wishes.

Tip 10
With your applications include articles that may have appeared in your local newspaper about you or your activities.

Tip 11
Include samples of your work that are extraordinary, or award-winning. Don't be afraid to send along copies of poetry, artwork, or even videos or cassette recordings of your special talents, which may include singing or dancing or playing the piano. Any special talent or hobby that you have, flaunt it. It makes your application stand out from others.

Tip 12

Many college admissions applications contain applications for financial aid as well. Therefore, whether you are applying for admission or a scholarship, pay close attention to all sections of an application because you have to be admitted to a college before you can win a scholarship sponsored by it.

Tip 13

Applications should be turned in as far in advance as possible. There are many scholarships issued on a first-come, first-served basis. Once the funds are depleted, you cannot apply until the following year.

Tip 14

Complete an application for financial aid. There are two primary financial aid forms, the FAFSA (Free Application for Federal Student Aid) provided by the government, and the CSS-FAF (College Scholarship Service Financial Aid Form). The CSS charges a fee for its service. Currently the fees are $13.75 for the first college they send results to and $9.75 for each additional college. The government FAFSA is free of charge. You should contact the schools you are interested in attending to find out which form they prefer. Generally, all of the above are acceptable. Even if you are not applying for a need-based scholarship, most college scholarship programs require you to have a copy of your financial aid statement sent to them. Again, even though you cannot officially file any of these forms until after January 1 of the year you plan to attend college, obtain one of the forms early and gather all the information you will need to fill out the form completely. For more information, refer to Chapter 2. The FAF will determine your eligibility for the following federal financial aid programs:

1. Pell Grant—Federal grant given to students who show financial need; amount is determined by the depth of the student's need. This grant is usually the first form of financial aid a student must obtain before getting other types of federal aid and some scholarships. For this reason, many scholarship programs require you to fill out the FAF when applying for their scholarship, especially if the scholarship is a need- rather than a merit-based scholarship.

2. Federal Supplemental Educational Opportunity Grant (SEOG)—Given in addition to the Pell, this grant is awarded to students who have extreme financial need; amount is determined by the institution you attend. Most schools deplete their SEOG funds early, so it is imperative that you complete the FAF as soon as possible.

3. College Work-Study—A part-time job at the college or university you attend that pays you money to offset your educational expenses.

4. Stafford Loans—Students who show financial need are eligible to borrow money from banks and other financial institutions, with a state governmental agency usually serving as a guarantor for the loan.

5. Perkins Loans—Students who show financial need and who are enrolled in a participating school are eligible to participate in this federal loan program, in which the loans come directly from the government.

To be eligible for federal financial aid you must:

1. Be a U.S. citizen or an eligible noncitizen.
2. If you are male you must be registered by the Selective Service.
3. You must show financial need.
4. You must attend a school that participates in federal financial aid programs.
5. You must be working toward a degree or certificate.
6. You must be making satisfactory academic progress.

7. You must not be in default on a federal loan or owe a refund on a grant.

If you gather the information you need early and acquire the FAF ahead of time, then as soon as your parents receive their W-2 forms you can send it off. If eligible, early applications receive the money first, as is the case with the SEOG mentioned previously in this chapter. All applications should be submitted by May 1 of the year you plan to enter college. Scholarships sponsored by private organizations usually do not require a financial aid statement, but they may require a copy of your parent(s') W-2 forms.

Copy the entire FAF once it is completed. When the Student Aid Report (SAR) arrives you must verify your information on the FAF. Keep all documents used to complete the form. Some schools have a verification process and may require you to submit copies of supporting documents. All applications must be filed by May 31. For Pell Grants and other federal financial aid, you must reapply each year. The SAR, which you will receive after applying for financial aid, must be submitted to the financial aid office of the institution you plan to attend by June 30 of the year you plan to enroll.

To determine what will be your expected family contribution, and for an idea of how much federal financial aid you will receive, write the Federal Student Aid Information Center, P.O. Box 84, Washington, D.C. 20044, or call (800) 433-3243.

Tip 15

As a part of the application process you may also be required to submit a graded writing sample from your English class. Discuss this with your English teacher so you can select the best sample of your writing. Writing samples should express a clear, concise writing style that reflects your viewpoint.

Tip 16

For questions that do not apply to you, write "not applicable" in the answer blank, or the abbreviated "NA," to show that you have not overlooked the question.

Tip 17

If you are not sure about the spelling of a word, look it up in the dictionary.

Tip 18

You may be required to list the names and addresses of your references. Some schools and scholarship programs ask for this so they can send recommendation forms to these individuals directly, without using the student as a medium.

The following questions frequently appear on college applications. They will help you prepare for filling out multiple applications in the future. If you cannot type and plan to have someone type your applications for you, it will help them tremendously if you have the generalized information handwritten neatly and placed in a folder for them to use as a reference. Many of these questions are basic, but answering them may require time and a little research, especially queries relating to other family members.

THE MOST FREQUENTLY ASKED QUESTIONS ON COLLEGE APPLICATIONS

- In what semester or quarter do you plan to enroll? This question is asked on all college applications; it basically establishes what class you will be in and the period for which you will need financial assistance.
- What is your state of legal residence? If you are a resident of the state in which this institution is located, in what month and year did you become a resident?
- What is your intended program of study and major?
- If you have previously attended the institution to which you are applying, what were the dates you attended?
- If you graduated prior to June of the year you are applying to enter the college or university, give an explanation of how you spent the time in between (refer to Chapter 7).

- What are the dates you took or plan to take the SAT and ACT?
- What is your Social Security number?
- In which country are you a citizen? If you are a legal alien, what is you registration number?
- Give a description of your academic honors (refer to Chapter 5).
- Give a description of your extracurricular and personal activities (refer to Chapter 5).
- What activities do you plan to participate in during college?
- What courses are you currently taking in high school?
- State the names of both parents, their addresses, occupations, and highest level of education completed. If either one attended college, what is the name of the college(s) they attended?
- What are your birthdate and place of birth?
- What are the name and address of the high school you are currently attending?
- What are the name, address, and denomination of the church you are currently attending?
- What are the name and telephone number of your high school guidance counselor?
- What is the college board number of the high school you will graduate from?
- Have any family members ever worked for this college or university? If so, list their names, dates of employment, and their relationship to you.
- List the names of any brothers and sisters, their ages, and the colleges they attended.
- What languages other than English do you speak?
- What is your first language?
- If you have taken the SAT and the ACT, list the dates and your scores. If you have not, have you registered to take them? On what dates?
- What is the class size and your rank in that class (refer to Chapter 3)?

- Do you have any physical limitations that require special assistance and consideration?
- Do you have, or have you had in the past, any emotional problems that would affect your educational performance?
- What is the name of your hometown newspaper?

THE MOST FREQUENTLY ASKED QUESTIONS
ON SCHOLARSHIP APPLICATIONS

1. What is the size of your graduating class, and what is your rank in it?
2. To which schools have you applied? What are the dates that you applied?
3. What schools have accepted you as a student?
4. What is your current grade point average?
5. What is your mother's annual income?
6. What is your father's annual income?
7. How many dependents are in your family?
8. How many members of your family are in college?
9. What degree do you intend to pursue in college?
10. Do you work? What is your annual income?
11. Please list all money available for college expenses.

Scholarships	$_____
Grants	$_____
Savings	$_____
Parents	$_____
Other (_____)	$_____

When you estimate these amounts, do not include scholarships that come from colleges or universities unless you are certain of your college choice. Receipt of some National Merit and National Achievement Scholarships depends on your college choice and your intended major. Unless you are certain your scholarship will "travel" to whichever school you choose and with any major, do not include it.

If the SAR shows that you are eligible for a Pell Grant, do not include the Pell Grant amount; these grants are funneled through the school, and even though you may be eligible for the maximum amount you may not receive it. You may also be asked for the date you filed the FAFSA, CSS-FAF, and other financial aid forms.

In addition, you may wish to prepare a statement of financial hardship to explain any extenuating circumstance(s) that would prohibit you or your family from contributing to your educational expenses. This statement should be written in essay format. You should send this statement along with your application for financial aid if you are applying for a need-based scholarship from a particular college or university. Do not hesitate to call a particular college or university that you are extremely interested in attending to inform the institution that unfortunately you cannot afford to attend because the financial aid package they have offered you cannot meet your needs. Some schools may reconsider, especially if you are an exceptional student.

Many scholarship programs also want you to estimate your total college expenses. The information in the table on page 65 is based on the average expenses in 1993 for a full-time student enrolled in a four-year college or university.

	PUBLIC COLLEGE/UNIVERSITY	PRIVATE COLLEGE/UNIVERSITY
Tuition	$1,700	$12,000
°Room	$1,000	$ 4,000
†Board	$1,400	$ 2,000
Books	$ 500	$ 500
Miscellaneous and Personal Expenses	$ 800	$ 800
Transportation	$ 350	$ 350

The amounts listed above are estimates. Actual amounts could be more or less, probably more. For a better assessment of your college/university expenses, look at the catalogs of the various schools you are interested in and use the information you find to calculate a more realistic estimate. If you do not have the current catalog, call the admissions office and ask about the cost of tuition and room and board for a year. Personal, transportation, and miscellaneous expenses are variable costs and depend solely upon your needs. Do not inquire about these items. The amounts listed in the preceding table should suffice if you cannot reach an estimate on your own. The cost of books also varies, but most institutions should be able to give you a general average.

° *Room* refers to the amount you will need to stay in the dormitory or campus housing without the benefit of meals.

† *Board* is the amount you will need for meals from the college or university cafeteria.

Perfection is a state of mind—yours and theirs.

———————

Anonymous

◆

7

WRITING PERFECT ESSAYS

$\boldsymbol{\mathcal{W}}$riting essays is one of the most essential components of your scholarship search. So, learning to write a good essay is important to your success. Essay composition is required for most college and private scholarship applications. The images created with words and the values revealed in essays that are submitted to scholarship programs are often elemental to their selection of scholarship winners. In fact, there are many scholarship competitions that are based solely on the quality of your essay.

The main purpose of essays is to give an in-depth view of you as a unique individual. Most essay questions are designed to help evaluators discover the values, ideals, achievements, and traits that make up your personality. Therefore, a well-written essay may give evaluators a glimpse of your inner self through your ability to write a cohesive, well-thought-out writing sample. An essay can also explain any special circumstances which may have had an impact on your life. For instance, if you have had a period in school in which your academic performance was less than satisfactory, write an essay explaining why and include it with all your applications. Many scholarship committees will ask for an explanation if this circumstance applies to you.

An essay can achieve one of two major objectives for you. In conjunction with your application, extracurricular activities, and academic record, an essay can make scholarship administrators eager to meet the person behind the words. This will result in advancing you to the next stage of competition, an interview. An essay can also compel scholarship administrators to reward you for your outstanding effort and make you one of their scholarship recipients. You can fulfill these objectives by making the content of your essay interesting, insightful, and informative.

Scholarship programs are looking for essays that show clear thought patterns, creativity, enthusiasm, and potential. Exhibiting these qualities accurately and uniquely is essential to the effectiveness of your essay as a tool to win scholarships. Essays prepared for competition of any kind need to capture their readers' attention and stand out from other essays. The best way to accomplish this is to use honest, straightforward prose and be true to your natural voice. In addition, you should ensure that your essay is well presented in an attractive format that is easy to read and pleasing to the eye.

To accomplish this you should make the overall presentation of your essay and application look as neat and professional as possible. If you have a word processor or, even better, a computer with a page-layout program such as Microsoft Word for Windows, Pagemaker, or Ventura Publisher, use it. Graphic elements will enable you to have an edge over the other applicants. But keep in mind that fancy layout can only complement the content of your essay, not compensate for lack of skill.

For writing essays I have found that the basic five-paragraph essay format is a winner every time. For example, here is a simple outline for an essay that can be jazzed up with unique variations.

Sample Outline for Essay Format

I. Introduction–One paragraph
   A. Use a quotation, poem, thought, amazing fact, idea, question, or simple statement to draw your reader into your topic.
   B. The main idea does not have to be stated in the first sentence, but it should definitely lead to and be related to your main idea or thesis statement, which should intro-

duce three main points you will develop in the body of your essay.

   C. Avoid using statements such as, "I am going to talk about . . ." or, "This essay is about . . ."

II. Body—Three paragraphs

   A. Support the main idea with facts, thoughts, ideas, published poetry, quotes, and other intriguing, insightful material that will captivate your audience.

   B. Present clear images.

   C. If necessary, use a thesaurus to ensure that you are not using the same words repeatedly. Using a word over and over will become monotonous for your audience and distract them from your subject.

III. Conclusion—One paragraph

   A. Restate the main idea in an original way.

   B. You can again use a poem or quotation to leave an impression. However, avoid using this tactic in all three parts of the essay. It may appear repetitious and unoriginal.

   C. Refer to the future in terms of your plans pertaining to the subject of your essay. For example, in an essay describing your future career goals, refer to yourself in the career that you have outlined. This reference should project you, and the ideas you presented in the essay, into the future. Refer to the last paragraphs of the three sample essays for an illustration.

• Special Note—Using quotations or poems shows that you are well read and imaginative. Be selective and look for quotes that are enlightening and profound.

  Early in your scholarship search it is best to prepare two basic essays following the aforementioned format, which can easily be tailored to fit most scholarship application essay requirements. Most essays require descriptions of yourself and future career goals. Others may ask you to relate your most memorable experience or to describe the most significant person in your life. There is a list of typical essay topics at the end of this chapter.

WRITING ABOUT YOURSELF

When describing yourself in an essay, select three adjectives that characterize you or your values and support them by telling why these adjectives fit you and your attitude about life. These adjectives will make up the body of your essay and should be used as overall guidelines to provide unity and cohesiveness.

As you elaborate on the descriptive adjectives you have chosen, strive to show the following qualities in your essay:

- Sense of responsibility—Your essay should demonstrate your sense of responsibility and diligence. You may convey this by your involvement in extracurricular activities or through academic achievements.
- Participation in extracurricular activities—In the community and your high school, your out-of-school activities should exhibit initiative, leadership skills, and enthusiasm.
- Your potential for growth—Your essay should show how you have grown as a person from participation in extracurricular activities and how your growth could be an asset to the college or university you attend or would like to attend and in your community.

These qualities should be evident in every essay you write. Even if the essay is not a descriptive personal essay which characterizes yourself, it is still important to show your connection to these qualities.

There are three sample essays in this chapter. They are creatively written and reflect many of my ideals about the importance of education, the value of communication, and the responsibility of my generation to America. They were also scholarship-winners. It should be noted that each one incorporates some of the same parts, since after writing over thirty different essays I found that the principles of some essays could be easily substituted into another. Recycling is perfectly acceptable and could save you time and energy.

The following essays have been reprinted and analyzed according to the five-paragraph format and are presented to assist you in writing essays.

Future Career Goals

I wrote this essay first. The requirements were to write an essay about my future career goals in relation to a journalism scholarship. It revolves around my interest in journalism and describes chronologically how that interest blossomed from early childhood into my young adult years. Clear, original images are presented to reflect my love of journalism. In the conclusion I refer to the future in conjunction with my personal plans and ideals. For variety I added one additional paragraph.

I. INTRODUCTION

[1]**Throughout my life I have been involved in some unique activities, many of which have had to do with the areas of communications and journalism.**[2] Therefore, at an early age I began to develop a desire to pursue a career in one or both of these fields. This desire has progressed from elementary and middle schools into high school. Anchored to a foundation formed over a span of many years, its roots are now unshakable.

1. This is the introductory paragraph. I used this paragraph to introduce the main idea of the essay, the development of my interest in communications and journalism throughout my school career.
2. The sentence in bold print is phrased as a simple statement to lead the reader into the essay.

II. BODY

[3]The **building blocks of this foundation were laid**[4] in sixth grade when I began to participate in a weekly telecast at Walter P. Jones Elementary School. **As the primary newscaster as well as the student who compiled all the stories for the Jones Elementary news broadcast, I was fascinated by my work. It was challenging and exciting.**[5] As a result, while standing in front of a video camcorder my **passion for journalism and communications**[6] began. Throughout that year I participated in essay and oratorical contests, debates, and plays. My desire had taken firm root.

3. Supporting paragraph. It shows the development and origin of my interest in journalism and communications.
4. Imagery—Creates an image in the mind of the reader.
5. Presents facts to support the development of my interest. It also gives evidence of my responsibility and enthusiasm for my work.
6. Word-choice variety—I could have said, "my *interest* in journalism and communications began." *Passion* sounds more exciting and is apt to grab the reader's attention.

[7]Furthermore, in middle school I continued to compete in many contests involving these areas of interest. **The winning oration that I had written for the Optimist International Oratorical Contest (District Level) I recited along with several others on Channel 6, here in Macon, Georgia.**[8] **The seedlings of journalistic youth that had been planted in elementary school were mushrooming into boisterous young children of communicative creativity.**[9] **This quote by the English essayist Joseph Addison aptly described my feelings then and still does now: "Words, when well chosen and presented, have so great a force in them, that a description often gives us more lively ideas than the sights of the things themselves."**[10]

7. Supporting paragraph.
8. Presentation of fact.
9. Imagery.
10. Quote.

[11]As I progressed into my ninth-grade year in school, my interest in journalism and communications intensified. **Northeast High School encompassed a much broader scope than middle school because it contained the *Salmagundi* literary magazine, the *Golden Star* newspaper, and the *Valhalla* yearbook, which helped me gain experience in journalism as I became actively involved with an actual publication.**[12] **The children of communicative creativity had now become young adults of journalistic potential.**[13]

11. Supporting paragraph. Outlines the progression of my interests into high school.
12. Fact. This statement shows my potential for growth in this area and that I was aware of this growth.
13. Imagery.

III. CONCLUSION

[14]**I would like to pursue a career in journalism and/or communications because both areas, which are closely interrelated, have become an essential part of my life. Over the years this desire has grown like a sturdy young plant preparing to take over the world or me (whichever comes first).**[15] To me, communication is a marvel because it can open doors into worlds otherwise unknown. **Communication can transport you to the tombs of Egypt, the gold of Africa, or the green hills of Ireland.**[16] Through the power of words, spoken or read, man possesses the ability to convey anything.

14. The first two sentences restate the main idea and form the beginning of the conclusion.
15. Imagery.
16. Imagery.

[17]All of my experiences in writing and speaking have helped me to see the importance of communications; for example, in the field of broadcasting, where the presentation of information can influence and motivate. As a child, people and their attitudes provoked curiosity within my young mind. As a young adult, people, their attitudes, and their effect on our changing world fascinate me. Journalism and communications embrace both my curiosity as a child and my fascination as a young adult. **A career in either area would not only satisfy my goals but would hopefully make me an asset to my community, my state, and eventually the world.**[18]

17. Displays my growth in this area and my potential for future growth.
18. This statement exhibits my commitment to improving the society in which I live as it refers to the future.

What Can My Generation Do for America?

This essay was written after "Future Career Goals." As you can see, parts from that earlier essay were adapted for this one. This topic was specifically requested by a scholarship program for all its applicants. It is relayed in chronological order. I supported the main ideas with clear, original images, and concluded with references to the future. The essay supports the five-paragraph theme, and it includes a poem for variety.

I. INTRODUCTION

[1]**The generation of yesteryear was a generation whose eyes were opened by the dawn of technology and the age of profound change.** The generation of today is one grown accustomed to the passions of technology and one which has **quenched**[2] its thirst from the **wealth**[3] of new knowledge to be learned about the future. The generation of tomorrow, my generation, is one in which a new quest for knowledge will be **launched.**[4] Our **young minds are now bursting with poten-**

tial.[5] Yet our **mature minds will reap the harvest of wisdom**[6] that the generations of yesteryear and today planted in our thoughts as children and are still planting **as adulthood gradually steals away our carefree days.**[7]

1. Introductory paragraph and statement presenting an idea.
2. Word-choice variety.
3. Word-choice variety.
4. Word-choice variety.
5. Imagery.
6. Imagery.
7. Imagery.

[8]When we were born, my peers and I, we were born into a **country nipping at the heels of progress.**[9] All around us, things were changing rapidly, some changes destined for success, some unfortunately not. Unlike the children of generations before us, **our learning shifted from the responsibility of a few teachers to the new wonder that had appeared on the horizon, the almighty silicon chip.**[10] We began to learn many math and reading skills from the green computerlike screen of Speak'n'Spells and Speak'n'Maths, from companies such as Texas Instruments and many others which had picked up the gauntlet that had been flung to them by the new wonder chip. **We witnessed the arrival of home computers and video games. We enjoyed the pleasure of our own home movies made with the aid of video camcorders.**[11] We also witnessed the destruction caused by guns made more and more advanced. Our generation observed an entire **gamut**[12] of change and growth as we grew from childhood into the responsibility and awareness of young adults. **Therefore, my generation is one which is filled with the belief that as a country we must always be aware of reality. In essence, we should be aware of our weaknesses as well as our strengths.**[13] For example, in technology we are lagging behind like a runner in second place, so close to the one in front, often pulling ahead, but repeatedly

falling behind at different intervals in time. For America these intervals are not mere minutes, they are years. **My generation can breathe new life into the runner and then the pennant of America will once again stand upon a technological plateau envied throughout the world.**[14]

    8. Second introductory paragraph—This paragraph and the first paragraph are used to present facts, images, opinions, and ideas to introduce the main idea.
    9. Imagery.
  10. Fact.
  11. Fact.
  12. Word-choice variety.
  13. Main idea.
  14. Imagery.

II. BODY

[15]We must always be aware of the strengths of America. The bulk lies in its foundation, the generations of yesteryear and today; yet all foundations, no matter how sturdy, are dependent upon the rejuvenating additions of future generations. As a member of one of those generations, I would like to state what I hope will be my addition to the foundation of America. I plan to pursue a career in communications and/or journalism. **To me, communication is a marvel because it can transport you to the tombs Egypt, the gold of Africa, or the green hills of Ireland. Through the power of words, spoken or read, man possesses the ability to convey anything. A career in either journalism or communications would not only satisfy my goals as a productive member of my generation, it would make me an asset to my community, state, and country.**[16]

  15. Supporting paragraph.
  16. This section comes from the essay titled "Future Career Goals."

[17]Therefore, as a broadcast journalist I can help relate the ideas of our country by reporting and interpreting the concepts of technologists, lawyers, doctors, scientists, and the rest of our learned generation. The information that I present will have the power to influence and motivate the next generation, twenty years from now, and will eventually mold their contributions to America. My generation, as are the generations of yesteryear and today, is merely a reflection of the past and the efforts of our ancestors. A poem I wrote illustrates this statement.

Generations,
sprung from the vital tree of life,
its roots outspread, planted all over the world,
its branches extended throughout the seven continents
hovering over the broad expanse of sea, ocean, and lake,
its leaves,
some old,
clinging many years
finally fluttering to the ground to join the nests of
long ago
many,
existing on a plane which could only be termed the middle
suspended between the golden age of yesteryear
and rumblings of the future
and finally,
our generation,
the newly green buds of prosperity
noisy with the rustling of youth
gradually acquiring knowledge,
their freshness and vitality
a symbol of new life
and the herald of change.[18]

17. Supporting paragraph.
18. Poem inserted for variety. This is an original poem.

III. CONCLUSION

[19]**Therefore, it is the responsibility of my generation and generations afterward to expand our learning from history, forge new paths, and leave a trail for the generations of tomorrow to follow.** As our generation looks back on their lives, at the changes that have been wrought in our short lifetime, it seems as if we are living on a foreign soil. **Yet our country, which appears to be foreign land now, will seem to be the land of aliens in the future.**[20] Our children and subsequently their children will look on another period of rapid change and growth. **Cars which look like jets without wings at this point in time will be hovering if not flying in the air a few years from now.**[21] Also, like Russia who has one now, we will have fully equipped and manned stations in space. As a result of my generation many changes and improvements will be made. **Then, the runner America resembles will not be one flagging for want of breath, it will be one who has already won the race and has time to run back and help the others lagging behind.**[22]

19. Concluding paragraph which begins with restatement of the main idea.
20. Opinion.
21. Opinion.
22. This statement is an opinion, which presents an image and also refers to the future.

The Importance of Education

This essay was also a specific request by a scholarship program. Applicants were given three choices for topics and I picked this one because of its generality. In short, it could apply to anyone. In order to introduce this essay I began with a quote as a unique variation. It also incorporates parts of the two previous essays; this one I shortened to two paragraphs. The topic was adequately covered in the three hundred words required.

I. INTRODUCTION

[1]**"The true purpose of education is to cherish and unfold the seed of immortality already sown within us; to develop, to their fullest extent, the capacities of every kind with which God who made us has endowed us."**—John Franklin Jameson
[2]This quote successfully illustrates the value and importance of an education for everyone who inhabits this world. Therefore, it lends **credence**[3] to the idea that **education is the oil upon which we as well-run machines of humanity must operate.**[4] As innocent babies at birth, we begin with a new variation of an old product, the human being. As we grow and progress into adulthood, we continue to refine, rejuvenate, and contribute more and more to the product we were born with. For example, a statement by English poet George Herbert underlines this point. **"In doing we learn."**[5] As babies, as children, and eventually as adults, everything we do is a learning process, and as we mature we must continue to update and refine the information we have already absorbed as we travel the winding roads of life.[6]

1. Introductory quote.
2. Introductory paragraph and also a supporting paragraph.
3. Word-choice variety.
4. Imagery.
5. Quote.
6. Main idea.

II. AND III. BODY AND CONCLUSION COMBINED

[7]**When we were born, we were born into a country nipping at the heels of progress.**[8] In fact, since the dawn of time our world has benefited from the fact that mankind has the ability to adapt and educate. In time, education may eventually enable us to affect the entire universe in many ways. The generations of yesteryear have laid the basic framework. The generation of today must build upon it by continuing to keep our machines as well as our minds, the powerhouse of the machines, well

oiled with education. **Without education, and without the basic fundamentals of learning, mankind cannot operate nor can it prosper.**[9] Eventually humanity will fade away. **Therefore, it is the responsibility of my generation and generations afterward to expand our learning from history, forge new paths, and leave a trail for the generations of tomorrow to follow.**[10]

7. Concluding paragraph.
8. Statement regenerated from "What Can My Generation Do for America?"
9. Fact.
10. Main idea restated with a reference to the future.

SHORT ESSAY QUESTIONS

For some applications you will be required to answer several questions with short essays. Short essays are usually composed of no more than one hundred words and are generally required in conjunction with a full-length essay. They are primarily concise responses to specific questions on a designated area of the application. Usually you will find these types of questions on applications for competitions consisting of several levels. They can also be found on applications of admission for highly selective, prestigious colleges such as Harvard and Yale. Not only are these questions designed to reveal how effectively you can communicate your thoughts, but also how effectively you can communicate them in a concise and clear manner—hence the designated amount of space in which to write your short essay.

The key points to remember about responding to questions requiring short essays are to answer the questions thoroughly and to strive to keep an upbeat yet serious tone. Once you read a question, jot down possible items to include in your answer. Prioritize them and put the items that are most important at the top. Generally for these essay questions you will be required to answer them in the spaces allotted, so you may not be able to include everything you think of initially; hence the need for giving some items top priority. The most important concept to remember is to make statements that clearly reflect you. They should be cohesive in their entirety and also reflect a clear thought pattern.

The following are typical short-answer essay questions for many scholarship competitions and for some postsecondary institutions. The underlined items identify the areas in which I specified a major interest. The competition for which the essays were written was for students interested in communicative arts.

1. What have you accomplished in <u>communications</u> and <u>English</u> beyond regular classroom work?

In the area of communicative arts, my accomplishments have been wide and varied, mainly because my interests are broad. As captain and a member of the Academic Bowl Team, I study all subject areas for competition, especially literature. I have maintained an "A" average in English for all my school years. I am editor-in-chief of the award-winning *Salmagundi* literary magazine, in which I have been published for the past four years. In 1989, I won First Prize for Best Poem in the State at the Georgia Scholastic Press Association (GSPA) competition at the University of Georgia in Athens. Writing essays for contests is a hobby of mine, and I have won Third Place for an essay on Alexander Hamilton for the Daughters of the American Revolution (DAR) and First Place for one on Sidney Lanier. In the Optimist Club Oratorical contests, I have won First Place at the zone level for the past three years; I have repeated my speeches on television. As a member of the Fine Arts and Literary Team, I have been in productions for state contests and participated in reading clubs.

2. Make any statement in support of your selection which you think has not been covered elsewhere in your application.

Since I was a little girl, English has been a companion which has followed me. As a child it was a delight, as I revolved in a world of fairy tales, romance, and adventure. As a young adult literature has become an important bridge to good communication skills which I will utilize throughout my life. I am always writing stories and poems and speaking for contests as well as here at school. Currently I am researching John Steinbeck in terms of the fiftieth anniversary of *The Grapes of Wrath* for a feature article in the *Salmagundi* literary magazine.

The following lists are some common questions that are asked on scholarship applications for private organizations and colleges or universities. Many of them are seen on standard college and university admissions applications as well.

TYPICAL ESSAY TOPICS FOR SCHOLARSHIP APPLICATIONS FROM PRIVATE ORGANIZATIONS

1. Provide a personal statement.
2. Whom do you admire and respect the most? Why?
3. What activity or program is most meaningful to you? What are your reason(s) for getting involved?
4. What is the most interesting and profound book that you have read recently? Why?
5. What is the worst crisis or problem facing Americans today?

TYPICAL ESSAY TOPICS FOR COLLEGE/UNIVERSITY APPLICATIONS

1. Discuss a political, social, or economic issue that is important to you.
2. Comment on a recent scientific or technological advance and the impact it may have on the future.
3. Why did you choose _____ for a career?

4. Describe your ideal teacher.
5. What is the best advice you have received and why?

Checklist for Essay Perfection

1. Is your writing truthful and accurate?
2. Did you proofread your essay carefully?
3. Have you asked someone else to read it?
4. Is your essay neatly presented? (Double-spaced, printed on white bond paper, etc.)
5. Did you thoroughly respond to the essay question?
6. Do all the supporting paragraphs contribute to the overall theme of your essay?
7. Have you conveyed your enthusiasm in the presentation of your opinions and ideas?

Helpful Reference Books

Webster's New Collegiate Dictionary
Webster's New World Thesaurus
The Elements of Style, Strunk and White
The Admissions Essay, Power and DiAntonio
On Writing the College Application Essay, Bauld
Writing Your College Application Essay, McGinty (The College Board)
Writing Your Way into College, Ehrenhaft

It's better to be prepared for an opportunity and not have one, than to have an opportunity and not be prepared.

———————

Whitney Young

◆

8

SCHOLARSHIP INTERVIEWING TIPS

*Y*our research is done and your applications have been submitted—now it's time to prepare for interviews. For scholarship awards ranging from $50 to $1,000, usually nonrenewable, interviews are generally not required. However, for most college/university-sponsored as well as large corporate-sponsored scholarships an interview (sometimes more than one, depending on how steep the competition) is typically the final step. If you have made it to the interview stage you've probably managed to impress at least one person on the scholarship panel of interviewers.

Interviewers are primarily concerned with meeting with you to reinforce the image they have formed through your application, résumé, essays, and recommendations. In the interview stage interviewers mainly want to get the to know the person behind the words: *You.* Generally they want you to elaborate on items that stand out immediately on your application or résumé. For example, a line stating that you are an avid birdwatcher or that you helped with the presidential campaign for the current officeholder would attract attention. Items such as these are bound to raise questions. Be prepared to talk about yourself and any activities in an enthusiastic and professional manner.

Interviewers want to meet a self-confident, mature, articulate individual who will present a positive image as one of their scholarship recipients. Scholarship recipients are usually considered to be the "cream of the crop" at most universities. Therefore, most scholarship interviewers are looking for well-groomed and well-rounded students who will represent the organization or institution well.

WHAT TO WEAR

In speeches and seminars I have always advised scholarship interviewees to wear what their mothers or fathers wear to the office (unless they are totally outrageous). Wear what feels and looks comfortable on you yet still presents a professional image.

Gentlemen: Understated tie and jacket, dark shoes, possibly a preppy look, no earrings or excessive jewelry. Wear matching dress socks. Do not wear white athletic socks or socks in argyle or geometric patterns. No flashy, loud colors unless you're a clothes designer. If you dress the part, draw attention to this fact; don't let them think it's not deliberate. Do not wear tennis shoes. Polished, leather shoes are the most appropriate for interviews.

Ladies: Pale or dark muted colors, feminine suit or dress. Avoid flashy colors or designs. Hosiery should be flesh colored with no designs. No excessive jewelry or spike heels. Wear something classical, definitely not flamboyant, unless your future career goal is that of a designer. If you dress the part, make sure to draw attention to this fact so that your interviewers will know it's deliberate.

PREPARATION

Depending upon the stage of competition, semifinalist or finalist, and the amount of money involved, I have discovered a general pattern. The more money and prestige of a college/university or program, the more interviewers a program enlists. For large scholarship competitions that have several levels there is usually an average of four to six interviewers per interviewee.

The interviewee is usually invited into a midsized room and seated at one end of a table with interviewers flanking both sides facing you. If they give you time to relax and get your bearings, use it wisely and remember that they are not out to get you. All the interviewers I encountered were very nice. So be calm.

Tip 1

Interviewers usually ask questions about what you have written on your application or in your essays, so always review your copy before you go into an interview. Recommendations from teachers, counselors, and administrators are usually not mentioned, so don't be worried that they will bring up what was said about you. They are primarily concerned with you and your comments.

Tip 2

Be well versed about your activities and various roles you play in the community and in your school.

Tip 3

You should talk about your hobbies and special talents in a clear, knowledgeable manner. If asked, you should explain how you became interested in a particular hobby. If you profess to be a writer you should know about the subject and also have in mind a few writers you admire and the reasons why.

Tip 4

Whether or not you like to read or write, you should be able to name a favorite author or book in your conversation with the interviewer. Explain why a book or author is your favorite.

Tip 5

Be informed about current events. Form an opinion on prominent issues and have a solid basis for your standpoint. If one of the activities you list in your résumé is formal debating, some interviewers will attempt to debate a particular point with you.

Tip 6

The answers you give should be well thought out. When you are asked a question, take a few seconds to contemplate your response and then give a well-prepared answer. In addition, always try to use positive, decisive words. Take every chance possible to show your leadership skills, potential, and self-motivation in your answers. Approach questions as if you are giving an impromptu speech.

Steps for impromptu speeches include: restating the question; stating your position; giving two or three supporting points; and in conclusion restating the question and your position again. As you conclude an impromptu speech, clarify your statements and emphasize important ideas. Then reaffirm your answer.

Tip 7

Usually competitions requiring interviews last more than one day, and program administrators often give you a chance to meet your interviewers at a reception or in some type of informal setting. Don't miss the chance to talk to them, and if—and only if—you admire something they have done and it is public knowledge, don't hesitate to tell them why you admire their actions. Usually interviewers are public officials, published writers, or upper-level managers of corporations, so you may already know a little bit about them. If you have prior knowledge, try to use it to your advantage. Most scholarship programs don't tell you who your interviewers are before you arrive at a competition, but if they do, research your interviewers thoroughly if possible.

Tip 8

Relax. Remember, many of the interviewers themselves have gone through what you are going through, and they understand your feelings. Therefore, don't be so nervous that you can barely talk. If you have a dynamic application (which you should if you have followed the advice of this book) then the judges who interview you will go out of their way to make you feel comfortable, because after reviewing your application they are interested in the person behind the words.

Tip 9

Arrive at the interview site early. This not only demonstrates your enthusiasm and responsibility, it also eliminates the added nervousness that rushing causes. Arriving early will give you time to collect your thoughts and relax. Hence your demeanor will be calm and tranquil as you walk into the interview.

Tip 10

Wait until you are invited to sit down. If you are not, stand up for the entire interview.

Tip 11

Practice a firm handshake while looking the person in the eye. This conveys honesty, confidence, and respect.

Tip 12

Send handwritten thank-you notes to your interviewer(s) after the interview. The note should express your gratitude for the time he/she/they spent with you. It should also reaffirm your interest in the institution or program.

Tip 13

At the interview, look your interviewer(s) in the eye at regular intervals. Frequent eye contact is silent communication with the interviewer(s) that expresses your confidence and knowledge. Shifty eyes display dishonesty. A tendency to look at the ceiling shows unfamiliarity with a topic.

Tip 14

If you have brought along some of your work to show, place it on a table near you. If there is no table, place it by your side on the floor along with your handbag, if you have one.

Tip 15

Be pleasant and smile often.

Tip 16

Before the interview, eliminate unnecessary stressful activities. For example, if driving is stressful for you, do not drive to your interview. Also, avoid speaking with someone who habitually upsets you. Instead, talk to someone who always puts a smile on your face and has a positive attitude.

FREQUENTLY ASKED QUESTIONS
DURING AN INTERVIEW

- What would you contribute to the community of _____ College/University?
- In what activities would you involve yourself?
- Why would you like to attend _____ College/University?
- If you could do anything in the world right now, what would you do?
- Who's your favorite author? Why?
- If you could have dinner with him or her (your favorite author), what would you ask?
- Whom do you admire most in the world? Why? This person could be someone you haven't met but would like to.
- What do you see yourself doing in ten or fifteen years?
- What sets you apart from the other applicants?
- What will be your contribution to the world?
- What do you plan to do with your career as a _____?
- Is there anything you would like to add that we haven't covered?

＊Hint: Have a prepared statement for this part, because they almost always ask. If they don't, say that you would like to add something once they conclude their questions. At this point you should clear up any statements you might have made that sounded misleading and reiterate your leadership abilities, potential, and motivation. Memorize your connection with those qualities for all interviews.

Just over the hill is a beautiful valley,
but you must climb the hill to see it.

———————

Anonymous

◆

9

IT'S NEVER TOO EARLY TO PREPARE FOR THE SCHOLARSHIP SEARCH

*E*ven though it may seem a little early to begin searching for scholarships in the seventh or eighth grade, an early start will allow you to take advantage of many opportunities that will ensure college or university dollars for your future. For example, you can begin your research and gradually build up a database of scholarships that you will be eligible to apply for in your senior year. In addition, you have a chance to clearly outline your goals and plans for the future in terms of extracurricular activities and your academic record. Early preparation is a very important factor in a successful scholarship search. If you are prepared for the process before senior year, you will know exactly what to do and to which programs you should apply, and you will have a wealth of other knowledge. Early preparation creates two advantages: 1) You know what to expect; and 2) you are relaxed and calm about it. Prior knowledge and preparation are essential factors for success in any endeavor. To begin your journey in the seventh grade is to create a clear and virtually easy path for success.

When you prepare early you will have adequate time to write to numerous scholarship programs, perfect your essay writing and interviewing skills, participate and excel in various extracurricular activities, and also improve your SAT scores and your academic record. You should note that the largest scholarship programs, giving scholarships ranging from $4,000 to $30,000, have very early deadlines. For example, many of the deadlines fall in October and December of the applicant's senior year. Early preparation will increase your chances tremendously. It will also ease not only your mind but your parents' to have the scholarship journey well under way. So, start your scholarship journey as soon as possible.

While it is certainly true that the early bird often gets the worm, eleventh and twelfth graders should not count themselves out. Many battles have been fought, races have been won, and journeys successfully completed with self-motivation, determination, and persistence. Early preparation will definitely make any undertaking easier, but if you begin late it does not put you out of the running. A prime example of success in spite of a late beginning is myself. There were many elements that contributed to my scholarship success, such as a high academic record and participation in extracurricular activities throughout high school, yet I did not begin my scholarship journey, researching and writing letters, until the second day of high school in my senior year. So, you can be successful in spite of a late start, especially if you have a high level of self-motivation, determination, and persistence.

COUNTDOWN: THE SCHOLARSHIP CHECKLIST

Seventh, Eighth, and Ninth Grades
- When you enter high school you begin with a clean slate. Maintain that clean slate throughout your high school career. Scholarship administrators do not take kindly to suspension or expulsion from any school.
- You can begin to get involved in school and community activities such as the Beta Club, Science and Math clubs, or Academic Bowl teams. You can also become involved in the Red Cross or other youth community groups.

- If you are not involved in some activity within your church, you should become involved. Activities in the church, such as youth groups and the church choir, are considered extra-curricular activities and should be included on your résumé.
- Acquire a recommended reading list from an English teacher within your school or from the public library in your area. Reading books from this list will not only help to improve your verbal SAT scores, it will also give you something to talk about during scholarship interviews.
- Begin to participate in activities and contests such as essay contests, poetry contests, art exhibitions, drama productions, or oratorical contests. Participation shows that you are motivated, even if you do not win. It also enhances your communication skills, which will be useful during interviews and for writing essays. The more you participate and become involved, the more well rounded you will be as a person. Your participation will not only enhance your chances of getting a scholarship, it will also assist you in becoming a well-prepared and informed member of society.
- Review the track you are in for high school courses. Most high schools have three tracks of study: general, vocational, and college preparatory. Upon entering high school you must declare a track to follow throughout your education, according to your future plans. The general track is composed of courses for students who do not plan to attend college or vocational school after graduation. The vocational track is for students who plan to attend vocational school. The college preparatory track is for students who plan to attend a college or university. Most colleges and universities require you to have taken certain courses in preparation, hence the college preparatory track. These courses include four units of English, three units of science (with at least two lab courses), three units of math (algebra, trigonometry, and precalculus), three units of social studies (American history, world history, economics, and government), and two units of

one foreign language. Try to structure your schedule so that you can take these courses in addition to courses in fine arts, a third course in one foreign language, physical education, computer technology, and another laboratory course in science. Your counselor should be able to direct you in this area.

Tenth Grade

- Begin to familiarize yourself with standardized tests. Take the PSAT and the PACT. When taking these tests make sure to darken the *yes* oval so you can be included in the Student Search Service. Your participation in the Student Search Service will get you on the mailing lists of many colleges and will provide scholarship and academic information. The PACT also includes a questionnaire. Fill this out completely and honestly. Some colleges take their cues from the information you provide there, and the analysis will help you focus on your future career goals and college/university choices. After you receive your scores from these tests, carefully note your weak areas.
- Begin to run for offices in various clubs that you should already be involved in from your ninth-grade year. Start keeping a list of all activities and contests in which you have participated.
- Analyze your course schedule and the units you have already taken to see if you can take some advanced-placement courses. If you take the test given immediately after these courses and score high on it you can be exempted from college or university courses later, which is a savings in itself. The scores range from 1 to 5, with 5 being the highest score possible. A 3, 4, or 5 is usually acceptable for exemption from a course, subject to specific college and university requirements. Of course there is a charge for these tests, usually around $65.

Summer After Tenth Grade

- By now you should have begun to receive brochures and pamphlets from colleges. Keep these in your own personal file after you have read them carefully. Make special note of the ones that interest you. If you want more information send back the reply card or call the 800 number many colleges offer. Or you can request a college or university video. Most institutions will lend them to you for a short time. Some charge a small fee for allowing you to view them.
- If you are late on the scene, meaning you took the tests late and haven't received any scholarship information, your local library could be an excellent resource. Libraries generally have tons of information on numerous colleges, and most of these publications have addresses listed in them. If the library doesn't have enough information on the colleges you are interested in or scholarship opportunities that you may be eligible for, use the addresses and send off for more.

Eleventh Grade

- Take the PSAT again, even if you took it last year or the year before. This time it will qualify you for the National Merit/Achievement Scholarship Program with the appropriate scores. However, if you don't qualify for the scholarship competition you will still get practice for the SAT. This year you should take the SAT at least twice to become familiar with it. Make sure you take the time to read the booklets that come with the registration packet—and don't wait until the last minute to read them. Again, after receiving your scores, note your weak areas. Some schools prefer the ACT, so take that in your junior year also.
- Begin to finalize college/university choices.
- Start to attend college fairs in your area.
- Visit a college or university close to your hometown to get a feel for academic life.
- In your English classes, make sure you master the basic five-

paragraph essay format; this is the most efficient and the most effective for scholarship essays (see Chapter 7).

- Don't forget, in your junior year it's still important to stay out of trouble and remain involved in various activities in your community and school. Activities within your church are important as well.
- Keep entering contests; whether you win or lose, participation is important.

Summer After Eleventh Grade

- Go to the library and find books that list types of scholarships, grants, and monetary aid. Record the addresses and deadlines. Many of them are catalogued according to academic majors, ethnic groups, military affiliations, and private scholarships. Unless you are certain about your major, don't pick scholarships geared toward a specific career. Try to focus on general scholarships and list only those that apply to your ethnic group and interests. Refer to Chapter 1 for more information.
- If you choose to use a computerized scholarship service to get additional information, you should apply now to ensure that you receive the information before your senior year of high school begins. Refer to Chapter 1 for more information.

Twelfth Grade

- Take the SAT or ACT as soon as possible. If you can fill out the form the very first day that school opens, do so. Therefore, when you get your scores back you will have enough time to take the tests again if you aren't satisfied and will be able to send the later scores to the colleges of your choice.
- Complete a résumé of your activities and the awards you have won.
- Make your recommendations list of teachers and administrators.
- Write two basic essays based on the five-paragraph format.

- Complete a financial aid form as soon as your parents receive their W-2 forms.
- Visit colleges or participate in college/university tours. Go to a local college/university fair.
- Apply for admission to the colleges and universities that you have decided upon.
- Apply for scholarships from colleges and private organizations. If you receive acceptance letters from the colleges you applied to for early admission, send copies of the letters along with your scholarship applications for private organizations. Deadline dates are usually December 1, December 15, January 1, January 15, February 1, February 15, March 1, April 1, and April 15. The annual reply date to accept scholarships from colleges is usually on May 1st.
- Call radio and television stations. Many announce various community organizations' scholarship competitions.
- Wait and review your priorities for considering a college or university if offered a scholarship from one.

Don't waste life in doubts and fears;
spend yourself on the work before you,
well assured that the right performance
of this hour's duties will be the best preparation
for the hours or ages that follow it.

———————

Ralph Waldo Emerson

◆

10

I'M ALREADY IN COLLEGE—
ARE THERE SCHOLARSHIPS FOR ME?

*Y*es! There are definitely scholarships for students already in college. In some cases students who are enrolled in a college or university have a better chance at winning some scholarships, especially those that are college/university sponsored, mainly because of close proximity to the source of these scholarships. In addition, undergraduates and graduate students have numerous chances to get involved in organizations that sponsor scholarships. The National Society of Professional Engineers and the National Association of Black Accountants are two such organizations.

The primary focus of this book has been to help you realize that no institution or organization gives money without reason. Those reasons, along with general requirements such as meeting deadlines, can take the form of a dynamic interview, an outstanding personal narrative through an essay, a flawless and impressive résumé, and a complete application. These objectives can be achieved whether you are a high school senior, an undergraduate, or a graduate student. The primary keys to success in finding scholarships are preparation and determination. Therefore, the ideas I have presented in the previous chapters can apply at any stage of the educational process.

As I mentioned before, scholarship opportunities can be found within the college or university that you are attending.

Maintaining a close relationship with the career center and advisors at the institution will keep you apprised of those and other opportunities. You should also look within your major source of study, such as accounting or graphic arts, for funding to complete your education. Contact former places of employment for help as well. Corporations and businesses in the area you live may also be a viable source for financial aid. Review Chapter 1 for an extensive list of areas in which to inquire about financial aid resources. Below I have listed several programs that cater specifically to undergraduate students and graduate students. However, please do not overlook the addresses listed in Appendix A or the book titles listed in Appendix B. While many of the sources in the appendices may not fund or contain information for students already enrolled in a postsecondary institution, it would be beneficial to investigate those sources.

For graduate and professional financial aid applications, call 1-800-448-4631, or write to: Graduate and Professional School Financial Application Service, Box 2614, Princeton, NJ 08540.

For more information about graduate school financial aid opportunities, write to: Council of Graduate Schools, One Dupont Circle, Suite 370, Washington, D.C. 20036, or call (202) 296-8851.

Students who are enrolled in colleges and universities are expected to be more professional than high school students in their speech, manner of dress, and especially in presenting a résumé to an organization or career center for a part-time job, internship, or a scholarship. To present your list of achievements and qualifications, the following résumés are examples of what yours should look like. When you are applying for a job or an internship, include a one-page résumé. If you are applying for a scholarship to a scholarship committee, include the multiple-page résumé.

MARIANNE N. RAGINS

University Address
Florida A&M University
Box 71394
Tallahassee, Florida 32307
Telephone: (904) 681-9495

Permanent Address
P.O. Box 6845
Macon, Georgia 31208
Telephone: (912) 742-7195

Objective: Effective utilization of my extensive literary, analytical, and organizational skills for a major business entity.

Education: Presently matriculating as a junior at Florida Agricultural and Mechanical University's School of Business and Industry.

Major:	Business Administration
Expected Graduation:	April 1995
Grade Point Average:	3.88/4.0

Relevant Course Work: Honors English I and II; Principles of Economics I and II; Legal Environment of Business; Principles of Marketing; Intermediate Accounting I and II; Managerial Accounting; Quantitative Methods for Business Decisions I; Financial Accounting;

Achievements: Winner of more than $400,000 in scholarship awards; cover story, *Macon Telegraph*, May 2 and 4, 1991; national headlines, Associated Press, May 3, 1991; cover story, *Parade* magazine; featured in *Essence, Newsweek, Money, Jet, Reader's Digest, People, Black Enterprise*, and *YSB* magazines; appeared on *Good Morning America* (ABC), *The Home Show* (ABC), *Teen Summit* (BET); January 11 declared Marianne "Angel" Ragins Day in Wilmington, Delaware; Dean's List, Fall Quarter '91/Spring Quarter '92/Fall Quarter '92/Spring Quarter '93; Coca-Cola Scholar; Armstrong Scholar; Wendy's Scholar; National Dean's List, 1991–1993; Outstanding Service Award, 1991; Letter of Commendation from Thomas B. Murphy, Speaker of the House, Georgia General Assembly, 1991; Letter of Commendation from Clarence Thomas, Supreme Court Justice, 1991.

Organizations: Presidential Scholars Association; Phi Eta Sigma National Honor Society; University Honors Council; volunteer coordinator for Special Olympics, 1991; volunteer speaker at local middle and high schools; Red Cross volunteer; coordinator, Benjamin D. Hendricks Undergraduate Honors Conference, 1993 and 1994; panel speaker, "The 21st Century—Education Beyond the Classroom," 1993; Mock Trial Team, Florida Collegiate Honors Conference, 1992; Southern Regional Collegiate Honors Conference, 1991; international speaker at the Crystal Palace, Nassau, the Bahamas, 1993; Director of Organization and Planning, Hometown News; coordinating manager, Close-up.

Publications: Author and publisher (first and second editions) of *Winning Scholarships for College: The Inside Story*; national publisher for third and future editions is Henry Holt & Company, Inc., New York.

Work Experience:
06/93 to 08/93
EDS Belgium N.V.—*Overseas Internship Assignment in Brussels, Belgium*
- Assistant for the Sales, Finance, and Government divisions of EDS.
  Extensive involvement with the preparation of financial documents and sales presentations.

06/92 to 08/92
Electronic Data Systems (EDS)—*Internship Assignment in Raleigh, North Carolina*
- Proposal Manager
  Entailed managing and editing material from proposal and technical writers, coordinating staff meetings and project deadlines, as well as overseeing all aspects of production concerning the submission of EDS's proposal for the Tallahassee Integrated Public Safety System.
- Proposal Team Staff Member
  Desktop publishing, word processing, and production for various proposals.

Computer Proficiency: WordPerfect, Lotus 1-2-3, Ventura Publisher, Microsoft Word, MacDraw, Microsoft Excel, Microsoft Powerpoint, ABC Flowcharter, Photostyler, Freelance Graphics, Lotus Notes

References Available Upon Request

MARIANNE N. RAGINS

University Address
Florida A&M University
Box 71394
Tallahassee, Florida 32307
Telephone: (904) 681-9495

Permanent Address
P.O. Box 6845
Macon, Georgia 31208
Telephone: (912) 742-7195

Professional Objective: Effective utilization of my extensive literary, analytical, and organizational skills for a major business entity.

Education: Presently matriculating as a junior at Florida Agricultural and Mechanical University's School of Business and Industry.
Major: Business Administration
Expected Graduation: April 1995
Grade Point Average: 3.88/4.0

Work Experience:
06/93 to 08/93
EDS Belgium N.V.—*Overseas Internship Assignment in Brussels, Belgium*
Description of Work Assignment:
• Assistant for the Sales, Finance, and Government divisions of EDS
• Extensive involvement with the preparation of financial documents and sales presentations.

06/92 to 08/92
Electronic Data Systems (EDS)—*Internship Assignment in Raleigh, North Carolina*
Description of Work Assignment:
• Proposal Manager
Entailed managing and editing material from proposal and technical writers, coordinating staff meetings and project deadlines, as well as overseeing all aspects of production concerning the submission of EDS's proposal for the Tallahassee Integrated Public Safety System.

- Desktop publishing, word processing, and production for the following proposals:
  North East Ohio Information Network (NEOMIN)
  The City of Savannah
  The City of Broken Arrow
  Indianapolis Sewer System
  City of Indianapolis Collections System

Honors/Organizations:

COLLEGE

Dean's List—Fall Quarter '91/Spring Quarter '92/Fall Quarter '92/Spring Quarter '93
Phi Eta Sigma National Honor Society
Member of the University Honors Council
Presidential Scholars Association
Volunteer Coordinator for Special Olympics
Red Cross Volunteer
January 11 declared Marianne "Angel" Ragins Day in Wilmington, Delaware
Author of *Winning Scholarships for College: The Inside Story*
LGB Scholars Association

Professional Speaking Engagements

Department of Family and Children's Services—Fort Gaines, Georgia
James Farmer Scholars Program—Mary Washington College, Fredericksburg, Virginia
Positive Teens—Wilmington, Delaware
Delta Sigma Theta—Atlanta, Georgia
Keenan Program—Bethune-Cookman College, Daytona Beach, Florida
Crystal Palace—Nassau, the Bahamas

Certificates of Appreciation—Speaker

- Griffin Middle School—Tallahassee, Florida
- Havana Middle School—Tallahassee, Florida
- Bethel AME Church—Tallahassee, Florida
- Bethel Baptist Church—Tallahassee, Florida
- Northeast High School—Macon, Georgia
- Southwest High School—Macon, Georgia

- Church of God in Christ—Macon, Georgia
- Stubbs Chapel Baptist Church—Macon, Georgia
- Union Baptist Church—Macon, Georgia
- Regional Honors Convention—Roanoke, Virginia
- McEvoy Middle School—Macon, Georgia
- GED Graduation—Macon, Georgia
- Riverside Optimist Club—Macon, Georgia
- Regional Honors Convention—St. Augustine, Florida

May 2, 1991—front-page news story, *Macon Telegraph and News*
May 3, 1991—front-page story picked up by the Associated Press
May 4, 1991—front-page news story, *Macon Telegraph and News*
Appeared in articles for *Essence, Newsweek, Money, Jet, Reader's Digest, People, Black Enterprise, YSB*
September 17, 1991—cover story of *Parade* magazine

Television shows:
    May 6, 1991—appeared on *Good Morning America*, ABC morning news show
    June 14, 1991—appeared on the *Home* show, ABC home-improvement show
    Karla Heath Show
    Channel One News
    America's Best College Buys
    August 22, 1991—taping of *You Bet Your Life*, pilot game show starring Bill Cosby

Radio Shows:
    "Your Personal Finance with Charles Ross"
    WABC News
    WBZT News
    "Bob Laws Night Talk Show"

HIGH SCHOOL
- Academic Bowl Team
- Debate Team
- Drama Club
- Literary Team
- Math Club
- Math Team
- *Salmagundi* Literary Magazine

- Assistant Editor—Sophomore Year
- Co-Editor—Junior Year
- Editor-in-Chief—Senior Year
- Science Bowl Team
    - Captain—Junior and Senior Years
- Science Club
- Spanish Club
- Spirit Club
- Student Council
    President—Senior Year
- Quill and Scroll National Honor Society
- Mu Alpha Theta
- National Honor Society
- Macon Telegraph and News Teen Board
- Project Link
- Red Cross Youth Volunteer
- Y-Club
    Vice-President—1989–1990

Gold Medallion—First place, Optimist Oratorical Contest, 1987
Silver Medallion—Second place, Optimist Oratorical Contest, 1987
Second Place—(Oratory) Winter Forensics Forum, 1988
Bronze Medallion—Third place, Math Olympics, 1988
Certificate of Academic Achievement in Science, 1988
Certificate of Outstanding Achievement, 1988 and 1989
National Science Merit Award
Scholarship—Summer Journalism Workshop at the University of Georgia, 1989
"Best Poem in State," Georgia Scholastic Press Association, 1989
Plaque, "Best Bill," Georgia 44th Youth Assembly, awarded by the *Atlanta Journal and Constitution*, 1989
Black Youth and Business Entrepreneurship Program, Georgia College
Trophy—Science Bowl Regional Competition, 1989 and 1990
Trophy—Biology
Georgia Council Teachers of English Writing Award, 1989
Coordinator—Science Fair, 1989

Georgia Council Teachers of English Student Achievement Award, 1989 and 1990

Northeast Student of the Month—November 1989

Alternate for the Georgia Governor's Honors Program, 1990

Who's Who in American High School Students, 1990

National Leadership Service Award, 1990

National English Merit Award, 1990

Plaque—Project Link, Student Leadership Program, 1990

First Place Medallion—Optimist International Essay Contest, 1990

Trophy—Chemistry, 1990

Trophy—Outstanding Service Award, 1990

Northeast Observer for Model U.N., 1990

Delegate for Summit Conference on Bibb County Education, 1990

Black Georgia Scholar Award

Duval County Academic Invitational Tournament, 1989, 1990, and 1991

Certificate of Commendation—Regional Winner, Red Clay and Skyscrapers Georgia Alliance for Public Education, 1990

Georgia Certificate of Merit awarded by the State of Georgia, 1990

Letter of Nomination—Congressional Youth Leadership Conference, 1990

Champion Journalist, 1990

National Council of Teachers of English Writing Award, 1990

Published in *Minescape*, GCTE magazine

Letter of Commendation from Thomas B. Murphy, Speaker of the House, Georgia General Assembly, 1991

Letter of Commendation from Clarence Thomas, Supreme Court Justice, 1991

If you are applying for graduate school admission and scholarships, you will usually be required to submit a personal statement. This statement basically outlines your reasons for continuing your education beyond an undergraduate degree, and it touches on the experience you have acquired over the years either through working (Did you work for a couple of years before deciding to attend graduate school? Many schools will require at least two years of work experience) or activities during your undergraduate years (if you have decided to go to graduate school immediately upon receiving your undergraduate degree). The personal statement can also take the form of a response to a specific question, or it can be a basic descriptive essay about yourself. In either case, refer to Chapter 7 for more details on constructing responses in an essay format. The personal statement is similar to an essay. Its main objective is to convey a mature, professional view of yourself. It should reflect your intellect, academic goals, and self-growth gained during your undergraduate experience or as an employee. The following book will be very beneficial to you in constructing a personal statement.

*How to Write a Winning Personal Statement for Graduate and
    Professional School with Special Emphasis on Admission to
    Law, Business, and Medical Schools*
by Richard J. Stelzer
Peterson's Guides, Inc.
P.O. Box 2123
Princeton, NJ 08543

The following information includes a checklist for additional sources of financial aid at the undergraduate and graduate levels, and a list of addresses.

Checklist for Other Sources of Financial Aid

1. Magazines directed toward career and success-oriented people, such as *Black Enterprise*, *Money*, and *Fortune*.

2. Professors and other staff members at the college or university you attend. Many of them fund small scholarships themselves.
3. Read the college/university catalog to find out about fellowships, endowments, and scholarships.
4. Contact your local newspaper and the Chamber of Commerce.
5. Talk to your employer or manager.
6. Try to get a paid internship. Many corporations sponsor internship programs for undergraduate and graduate students. Some of them will also sponsor scholarships for interns who have performed well academically. Even if they do not fund all or part of the education of an intern, your job experience will enhance your résumé for future employment and scholarship consideration.

ADDRESSES FOR SCHOLARSHIP OPPORTUNITIES

American Institute of Certified Public Accountants for
 Minorities
1211 Avenue of the Americas
New York, NY 10036-8775

Association for Women in Science
Grants-at-a-Glance
1522 K Street, NW, Suite 820
Washington, D.C. 20005   (202) 408-0742

Bureau of Indian Affairs
P.O. Box 8327
Albuquerque, NM 87198

Coor Veterans' Memorial Scholarship Fund
Air Force Sergeants Association
P.O. Box 50
Temple Hills, MD 20748

Council on Legal Education Opportunity (CLEO)
Suite 290, North Lobby
100 M Street, NW
Washington, D.C. 20036   (202) 785-4840

Delta Sigma Theta Sorority, Inc.
1707 New Hampshire Avenue, NW
Washington, D.C. 20009   (202) 483-5460

Fellowship Office
National Research Council
2101 Constitution Avenue
Washington, D.C. 20418   (202) 334-2872

Kellog Foundation
400 North Avenue
Battle Creek, MI 49017

Leopold Schepp Foundation
15 East 26th Street, Suite 900
New York, NY 10010   (212) 986-3078

Mellinger Educational Foundation
1025 East Broadway
Monmouth, IL 61642   (303) 734-2419

National Association of Black Accountants
900 Second Street, NE, Suite 205
Washington, D.C. 20002

Realty Foundation of New York
551 Fifth Avenue
New York, NY 10017

Scholarships Foundation
P.O. Box 170
Canal Street Station
New York, NY 10013

Time Magazine College Achievement Award
c/o Media Management Services
10 North Main Street
Yardley, PA 19067   1-800-523-5948

Books
Free Money for Graduate Students
by Laurie Blum
Henry Holt and Company, Inc.
115 West 18th Street
New York, NY 10011

- Extensive listing of graduate scholarship opportunities.

*Getting Work Experience: The Student's Directory of
   Professional Internship Programs*
by Betsy Bauer
Dell Publishing Group, Inc.
1 Dag Hammarskjold Plaza
New York, NY 10017

- Lists the names of various corporations and the internship and
  training opportunities they have for undergraduate and graduate students.

Internships 1994
Peterson's Guides, Inc.
P.O. Box 2123
Princeton, NJ 08543-2123

- Comprehensive guide listing numerous paid and unpaid
  internship opportunities, including international internship
  programs.

All things are possible to him who believes.
They are less difficult to him who hopes.
They are more easy to him who loves,
and still more easy to him who perseveres
in the practice of the three virtues.

———————

Brother Lawrence

◆

11

SCHOLARSHIPS FOR STUDENTS WITH SPECIAL NEEDS

*I*n addition to there being ample scholarship funds available to undergraduate and graduate-level students, there are scholarships specifically available for nontraditional students, such as individuals returning to college, international students, and those who are physically disabled. For specific scholarship strategies relating to these situations the methods discussed in previous chapters should be perused carefully, because they can apply here as well. The sources that follow cater to these circumstances.

• INSPIRATIONAL NOTE •

During a conference, I learned of a student who won one of the most prestigious fellowships sponsored by the U.S. government, the Truman Fellowship. This student had dropped out of school before reaching the eighth grade in order to work and help support his struggling family. With determination and perseverance he managed to obtain a GED, and he will soon graduate from a two-year community college. Upon his graduation he will receive the Truman Fellowship, worth approximately $30,000, to attend an institution of his choice to obtain his bachelor's degree.

SCHOLARSHIPS FOR STUDENTS RETURNING TO COLLEGE

Keep in mind that many colleges sponsor reduced- or nontuition programs for students returning to college which are subject to age requirements. Contact various colleges and universities of interest for more information.

Business and Professional Women's Foundation
BPW Career Advancement Award
2012 Massachusetts Avenue, NW
Washington, D.C. 20036   (202) 293-1200

MENSA
Rita Levine Memorial Scholarship Program
2026 East 14th Street
Brooklyn, NY 11235-3992

Society of Women Engineers
Olive Lynn Salembier Scholarships
345 East 47th Street, Suite 305
New York, NY 10017   (212) 705-7855

SCHOLARSHIPS FOR INTERNATIONAL STUDENTS

There are numerous scholarships for American students who want to study at colleges and universities abroad. Likewise, there are many scholarships and programs for foreign students who want to study at American colleges and universities. The following includes addresses and books for obtaining further information.

Council on International Educational Exchange (CIEE)
205 East 42nd Street
New York, NY 10017

Institute of International Education
809 United Nations Plaza
New York, NY 10017

Office of International Training
Washington, D.C. 205233

Books
   The Encyclopedia of Associations—International Organizations, Part I—Descriptive Listings
Gale Research, Inc.
835 Penobscot Building
Detroit, MI 48226-9948   1-800-234-1340

• Volume of descriptive listings for international organizations that support and foster international studies.

A Foreign Student's Selected Guide to Financial Aid Assistance for Study in the U.S.
Adelphi University Press
South Avenue
Garden City, NY 11530

• This guide helps international students discover various sources of financial aid.

Global Guide to International Education
David Hoopes, Editor
Facts on File Publications
460 Park Avenue South
New York, NY 10016

• Comprehensive guide of organizations, corporations, special programs, and other sources that assist students with the expenses of obtaining an international education.

SCHOLARSHIPS FOR DISABLED STUDENTS

Most disabled students are eligible to receive aid from the federal government, as are disabled veterans and students who are legally blind.

American Council of the Blind
1010 Vermont Avenue, NW, Suite 1100
Washington, D.C. 20005   (202) 393-3666

American Foundation for the Blind
15 West 16th Street
New York, NY 10011   (212) 620-2043

Bell Association for the Deaf, Inc.
3417 Volta Place, NW
Washington, D.C. 20007   (202) 337-5220

Foundation for Exceptionally Gifted Children
1920 Association Drive
Reston, VA 22091   (703) 620-1054

Gore Family Memorial Foundation Trust
230 Southeast First Avenue
Fort Lauderdale, FL 33301   (305) 462-6643

National Technical Institute for the Deaf
Lyndon Baines Johnson Building
Rochester, NY 14623-5603   (716) 475-6400

Special Education and Rehabilitative Services
330 C Street, Room 3028
Washington, D.C. 20202-0001   (202) 732-1265

Special Services Branch
Division of Student Services
Box 23772
L'Enfant Plaza Station
Washington, D.C. 20026-3772

Vocational Rehabilitative Services
330 C Street, Room 3028
Washington, D.C. 20202-0001   (202) 732-1282

Books
Financial Aid for the Disabled and Their Dependents
by Gail Ann Schlachter
Reference Service Press
3540 Wilshire Boulevard, Suite 310
Los Angeles, CA 90010

• This book lists financial aid sources for disabled students and
  their dependents.

*Guide to Colleges with Programs or Services for Students with
Learning Disabilities*
by Midge Lipkin, Ph.D.
Schoolsearch
127 Marsh Street
Boston, MA 02178

• This book lists numerous colleges with programs for students
  with learning disabilities.

I find the greatest thing in this world not so much where we stand, as in what direction we are moving. To reach this port of heaven, we must sail sometimes with the wind, and sometimes against it but we sail, and not drift, nor live at anchor.

Oliver Wendell Holmes

◆

12

MAKING CHOICES

*C*ongratulations! You have received a scholarship award letter. Usually you need to formally, in writing, accept or reject the offer by May 1 of the year you plan to begin your postsecondary education. This date is the national scholarship deadline.

The following are items you may want to consider before choosing a scholarship offer, regardless of how much money they are offering. These considerations are divided into two categories: Category A for scholarships from a particular college or university, and Category B for scholarships from private organizations.

Category A—Scholarships from Colleges or Universities

- Is it a full or partial scholarship? If partial, what does it cover?
- Are there any other incentives to "sweeten the pot" other than the scholarship itself? For example, some "sweeteners" are living stipends, a personal computer for your academic use, internships with companies in your particular area of study, summer study-abroad programs, a private dormitory room, and the like.
- Is there a graduate feeder program? Can this institution help you get a scholarship, fellowship, grant, or other financial aid to afford graduate school if you need it?

- What will the degree you receive from this particular college or university prepare you for?
- Will the educational benefits from this institution fulfill your postsecondary educational goals?
- How are other graduates faring after they leave the institution?
- Are there many students transferring out of the institution, particularly scholarship students?
- What type of overall reputation does the institution have?
- Will you receive the attention you need to thrive at this institution? Is it a large university with an impersonal environment in an urban area, or is the college small, with an intimate atmosphere in a little town?
- What types of special arrangements are made for scholarship students? For example, some arrangements are honors programs, special advisors, student support groups, special dormitories, fraternities, and sororities.
- What is the average class size?
- Is on-campus housing available for four years or more of your college career, or are upperclassmen expected to move off-campus to allow room for incoming freshmen? If upperclassmen are expected to move into off-campus housing, will the scholarship pay for this arrangement?
- Do you want to attend this college or university regardless of the scholarship or financial aid it offers?
- How many nonmajor courses are required?
- What are the hours for the library and computer rooms?
- Are the library and computer facilities adequate for the entire student body?
- What is the job placement rate of graduates from this college or university, especially in your intended major?
- How many years does it take the average student to graduate? How many years does it take the average student to graduate in your intended major? Measure these years against the time your scholarship will cover.
- What situations could result in temporary or permanent suspension of the scholarship?

- What grade point average do you need to maintain to keep the scholarship?
- What is not covered by this scholarship offer? For example, summer school courses, books, room and board, any courses over those allotted to be considered a full-time student, courses that must be repeated, any books that must be purchased off-campus and not at the campus bookstore, and similar factors.
- Even with the aid of a full scholarship, can you afford to attend the college of your choice? What additional assistance will you need? For example, examine the cost of living in the city where the college is located. Try to uncover hidden costs.
- Are off-campus classroom sites a regular occurrence for courses in your intended major? If so, it will add to your basic transportation costs.
- Are the costs of lab materials covered in your scholarship? In many cases they are not. Since most schools require at least two basic science courses such as physics or chemistry with corresponding labs, this can be a hidden cost.

Here are some things you should do to help answer some of your questions about a particular institution.

- Talk to other students at the school, especially scholarship students. Talk to an alumnus. Many schools will have students and also parents call you at your home. Take the time to jot down general questions about your interests and keep it by the phone for these instances.
- Visit the campus. Speak to students, especially those in the library. These students tend to be more serious about their work and usually won't have the bias of failing grades to color their views or comments. Talk to the professors. Spend the night in the freshman dormitory. Eat in the cafeteria.
- Look at course offerings for required classes and those for your intended major. Look at the sections available each semester or quarter. With the excessive budget cuts

lately, many schools are cutting down on the number of courses and the sections for each course. This may cause a problem when the unavailability of a course could mean an extra semester, quarter, or year in school without financial backing from your scholarship.
- Visit the admissions office. Inquire about the dropout rate and the reasons for students leaving.
- Talk to personnel in the career center, if the school has one.

Category B—Scholarships from Private Organizations

- Is it a full or partial scholarship? If partial, what does it cover?
- What situations could result in temporary or permanent suspension of the scholarship?
- What grade point average do you need to maintain to keep the scholarship?
- Will the scholarship "travel"? For example, do you have to attend a specific institution to receive the scholarship? Also, will you have to major in a particular discipline to keep the scholarship?
- What type of support system does the scholarship program have for its scholars?
- How will the funds be transferred to the institution you want to attend? Some scholarship checks do not arrive before the student has to meet the financial obligations at the school he or she plans to attend.

Wonderful! You have successfully completed your scholarship journey. Many of the skills such as research and interviewing techniques that you sharpened and honed while using this book will aid you throughout life, especially in college. I hope the hours of research, writing letters, taking tests, interviewing, and the many other activities that went into your search have resulted in numerous scholarships that will allow you to thoroughly enjoy your college experience.

College can be one of the most exciting and rewarding experiences in your life. Not only is it possible to tap into a wealth of knowledge from a variety of people while on campus, you can also meet the friends of a lifetime. The experience that can be gained only through a college education is definitely worthwhile. As a student on a campus surrounded by professionals and intellectuals, you can build a network of influence and knowledge to draw from as you begin to search for a job, start your own business, or undertake other ventures.

The decision to enhance your education by attending college is one of the best choices you can make. As our world careens toward extremely technological societies, education beyond high school becomes more important each and every day. An advanced education is an important tool with which to fashion the lifestyles that many of us would like to enjoy. In fact, life itself is a continuous learning process. For those of us who choose to embrace education, learning everything we can, whenever we can, there are infinite opportunities that await us.

By choosing to pursue a college education and securing the scholarship funds to implement it, you are embarking on another exciting journey, much like the scholarship journey, which will reward you throughout your life. I wish you much success in all your endeavors. Most important, enjoy your life and strive to take advantage of every opportunity that comes along.

APPENDIX A

Abbreviated List of Scholarship Programs

The following is an abbreviated list of scholarship programs that I compiled in my search as a high school senior, and while helping my brother, Travis, in his scholarship search. Under no circumstances should this partial list take the place of individual research. Many of these programs may not be available where you reside. Although the addresses listed here are mainly for graduating high school seniors, many of the programs at these addresses administer scholarships for undergraduate and graduate students as well.

Alpha Kappa Alpha
5656 South Stony Island
Chicago, IL 60637

American College Scholarship
  Program
419 Lentz Court
Lansing, MI 48917

American Society of Military
  Comptrollers
Middle Georgia Chapter
Box 512, South Base Branch
  Post Office
Robins Air Force Base, GA
  31098

Armstrong World Industries, Inc.
Personnel Department
P.O. Box 3001
Lancaster, PA 17604

Arts Recognition and Talent
  Search
300 Northeast 2nd Avenue
Miami, FL 33132

The Bell Honors Program
Professor G. Hewett Joiner,
  Director
Campus Box 8054
Georgia Southern University
Statesboro, GA 30460-8054

C&S Sovran Trust Company
Jacques Scholarship Fund
P.O. Box 4007
Macon, GA 31213

Career Opportunities Through
    Education, Inc.
Service Merchandise
    Scholarship Program
P.O. Box 2810
Cherry Hill, NJ 08034

Citizen's Scholarship Foundation
    of America
P.O. Box 88
St. Peter, MN 56082°

Coca-Cola Scholars Foundation,
    Inc.
One Buckhead Plaza, Suite 1000
Atlanta, GA 30305

College Board Admissions
    Testing Program
P.O. Box 6200
Princeton, NJ 08541-6200

Converse College
Honor Scholarship Program
Spartanburg, SC 29301

Daughters of the American
    Revolution Scholarship Funds
1776 D Street, NW
Washington, D.C. 20006

Duke University
2138 Campus Drive
Durham, NC 27706

Educational Communications,
    Inc.
721 North McKinley Road
Lake Forest, IL 60045

Elizabeth Tuckerman
    Foundation
P.O. Box 63954
San Francisco, CA 94163

Elks National Foundation
2750 Lakeview Avenue
Chicago, IL 60614

Fulfillment Systems, Inc.
Box 4000
Monticello, MN 55362

Guideposts
747 Third Avenue
New York, NY 10017

°The addresses listed for the Citizens' Scholarship Foundation of America and
Scholarship Program Administrators, Inc., are clearinghouses for various scholarships
that they administer for several different private organizations. Write to these offices and
request a list of the scholarship programs they represent; ask them to include the
addresses.

The Herbert Lehman Education
Fund
99 Hudson Street
New York, NY 10013

Jackie Robinson Foundation
3 West 35th Street
New York, NY 10001

Kemper Foundation
Route 22
Long Grove, IL 60049

Lulac National Education
Service Center
400 1st Street NW, Suite 716
Washington, D.C. 20001

MENSA Scholarship Program
2026 East 14th Street
Brooklyn, NY 11235-3992

Minority Disadvantaged
Scholarships
The American Institute of
Architects
1735 New York Avenue, NW
Washington, D.C. 20006

Money College Guide
Sweepstakes
P.O. Box 60798
Tampa, FL 33660-0798

National Academy of American
Scholars
P.O. Box 7640
La Verne, CA 91750

National Association of Negro
Business and Professional
Women's Clubs
2618 Pinetree Drive
Flint, MI 48507

National Foundation for
Advancement in the Arts
800 Brickell Avenue
Miami, FL 33131

National Scholarship Trust Fund
Graphic Arts Technical
Foundation
4615 Forbes Avenue
Pittsburgh, PA 15213

National Society of Professional
Engineers
1420 King Street
Alexandria, VA 22314-2715

Pacific Gas and Electric
Company
77 Beale Street, Room 2825F
San Francisco, CA 94106

P.E.O. Sisterhood
3700 Grand Avenue
Des Moines, IA 50312

The Poynter Fund
Personnel Department
Times Publishing Company
P.O. Box 1121
St. Petersburg, FL 33731-1121

Presbyterian College
Presbyterian College
Scholarship Selection
Committee
Admissions Office
Clinton, SC 29325
1-800-476-7272

Rhodes College
Rhodes Scholarship Committee
2000 North Parkway
Memphis, TN 38112-1690

Sales Association of the
Chemical Industry
P.O. Box 2148
287 Lackawanna Avenue, #A7
West Paterson, NJ 07424

°Scholarship Program
Administrators, Inc.
3314 West End Avenue,
Suite 604
Nashville, TN 37203-1022

Scholastic Writing Awards
Scholastic, Inc.
730 Broadway
New York, NY 10003

Science Service
1719 N Street, NW
Washington, D.C. 20036

Scripps-Howard Foundation
1100 Central Trust Tower
Cincinnati, OH 45202

Senior Publications, Ltd.
P.O. Box 852
Wheatley Heights, NY
11798-9804

Shell Oil Companies Foundation
Two Shell Plaza
P.O. Box 2099
Houston, TX 77001

Society of Mining Engineers
Secretary
P.O. Box 625002
Littleton, CO 80162-5002

Society of Women Engineers
Scholarship Program
345 East 47th Street
New York, NY 10017

Stanley M. Sprague Memorial
Scholarship Committee
New Hampshire Conference
United Methodist Church
Box 385
Concord, NH 03301

Tylenol Scholarship Fund
1675 Broadway, 33rd Floor
New York, NY 10019

°The addresses listed for the Citizens' Scholarship Foundation of America and Scholarship Program Administrators, Inc., are clearinghouses for various scholarships that they administer for several different private organizations. Write to these offices and request a list of the scholarship programs they represent; ask them to include the addresses.

United States Jaycees
P.O. Box 7
West 21st Street
Tulsa, OK 74121

U.S. Air Force Academy
Colorado Springs, CO 80840
(719) 472-1818

U.S. Military Academy
West Point, NY 10996
(914) 938-4011

U.S. Naval Academy
Annapolis, MD 21402
(410) 267-6100

Waffle House Foundation
P.O. Box 6450
Norcross, GA 30091

Youth Foundation
36 West 4th Street
New York, NY 10036

Zeta Phi Beta Sorority, Inc.
1514 North 25th Street
Baton Rouge, LA 70802

Books and Periodicals
for Scholarship Reference

This is a partial listing of books and magazines that may prove helpful in your scholarship research efforts. Look for them in your local bookstore or library, or order them from the addresses shown.

BOOKS

The College Blue Book
Macmillan Publishing Company
866 Third Avenue
New York, NY 10022

- Comprehensive student financial aid listings.

College Costs and Financial Aid Handbook 1994, 14th Edition
College Board Publications
Box 886
New York, NY 10101

- This book helps students and parents estimate the costs of attending college. It is also a guide to figuring out how to meet the estimated costs.

College Funding Made Easy: How to Save for College
While Maintaining Eligibility for Financial Aid
by J. Grady Cash
Betterway Publications
P.O. Box 219
Crozet, VA 22932   (804) 823-5661

• Financial aid planning book.

Dollars for Scholars
by Marguerite J. Dennis
Barron's Educational Series
113 Crossways Park Drive
Woodbury, NY 11797

• Guide to student financial aid.

Free Money for College
by Laurie Blum
Henry Holt and Company, Inc.
115 West 18th Street
New York, NY 10011

• Student financial aid listings.

How to Obtain Maximum College Financial Aid
by Edward H. Rosenwasser
Student College Aid Publisher
2525 Murworth, Suite 207   (713) 668-7899
Houston, TX 77054   1-800-245-5137

• This is a step-by-step guide to completing financial aid forms, as well
  as a comprehensive listing and explanation of scholarships, fellowships, loans, and grant opportunities in the areas of health, law,
  business, and other fields of interest.

How to Pay for Your Children's College Education
by Gerald Krefetz
College Board Publications
Box 886
New York, NY 10101

- This book is for parents looking for investments to pay for their children's college education.

The National Directory of Addresses and Telephone Numbers
Omnigraphics, Inc.
Penobscot Building
Detroit, MI 48226   1-800-234-1340

- Comprehensive list of the addresses and telephone numbers for all registered foundations, associations, corporations, and many other organizations within the United States.

Panic Plan for the SAT: How to Score Your Best at the Last Minute
by John Davenport Carris with Michael R. Crystal and William R. McQuade
Peterson's Guides, Inc.
P.O. Box 2123
Princeton, NJ 08543-2123

- Designed for students who have waited until the last minute to begin preparing for the SAT.

The Scholarship Book
by Daniel J. Cassidy
Prentice-Hall, Inc.
Business and Professional Division
Englewood Cliffs, NJ 07632

- This book contains an extensive and comprehensive listing of scholarship addresses.

The Scholarship Directory: 1992 Minority Guide to Scholarships and Financial Aid
Tinsley Communications, Inc.
100 Budge Street, Suite A-3
Hampton, VA 23669   (804) 723-4499

- Comprehensive listings of scholarships and aid for minorities.

PERIODICALS

Money

- *Money* magazine is published monthly and usually has several self-improvement articles in addition to a special issue which is devoted to students and their college aspirations. The special college issue has numerous advertisements from businesses willing to aid families in drafting financial plans. *Money* also has an annual list of colleges that give out the largest scholarship and financial aid packages.

The Black Collegian
1240 South Broad Avenue
New Orleans, LA 70125

- This magazine will be especially helpful to undergraduate and graduate students who are seeking an internship or summer job. There are usually several articles aimed at professional development, such as interviewing techniques and résumé writing skills. *The Black Collegian* is published quarterly. Contact the magazine by mail if it is not available in your local bookstore.

Black Enterprise

- This is a magazine on black business enterprise. Published monthly, *Black Enterprise* will be especially helpful to the undergraduate or graduate student looking for a summer job or internship.

Private Colleges and Universities
Carnegie Communications, Inc.
750 Third Avenue
New York, NY 10017   (212) 682-7483

- This magazine is aimed toward spurring minorities into pursuing a college education at a private college or university. It includes extensive profiles on colleges and universities (with tear-out postcards to order more information), as well as information about academic interviews, applications, and financial aid. The magazine also sponsors its own scholarship program. *Private Colleges and Universities* is published annually. Contact the magazine by mail or telephone if it is not available in your local bookstore.

USA Today
1000 Wilson Boulevard
Arlington, VA 22229   1-800-USA-0001

- *USA Today* is a daily newspaper that provides an annual information hotline for students who are interested in college. For questions about the availability of this hotline, use the customer service (1-800) number listed above. *USA Today* also sponsors a yearly scholarship competition.

Index